A typical scene taken in the early nineteen sixties, shows Browns Blue Bedford C5Z1 PUT 660, Bedford SB JNR 926, ex-LT RT HLW 144 and ex-LT RT HLW 151. **Photo/ Ken Jubb**

First published in 2012

ISBN 978 0 9569075 1 6

Published by Leicester Transport Heritage Trust Ltd., 13 Warren Road, Enderby, Leicester. LE19 2DR.

www.ltht.org.uk

AUGUST 2012

The author has spent nearly two years compiling information, photographs and all sorts of memorabilia to help with the production of this publication but that is only half of the story. Plans are being drawn up to commemorate the fiftieth anniversary of the last day of operation by Browns Blue, which takes place on Friday March 15th 2013; the last service run was operated at 10.25 p.m. from Marlborough Square, Coalville to Ibstock, on Friday 15th March 1963.

Unfortunately no former Browns Blue vehicles have survived, but a surprising number of former London Transport AEC RT double deckers of the type that Browns operated are still in existence, many have been exported overseas, however those that have survived in this country are gradually being returned to their original condition by enthusiasts who after many years of expensive restoration work are reluctant to part with their pride and joy, this makes it almost impossible to acquire such a vehicle, but not quite!

After many months of searching, I finally answered an advert in a bus preservation magazine and purchased KLB 596 formally RT 1347, this vehicle is very similar to the nine former London Transport AEC RT buses purchased by Browns in 1958. It has been refinished in "Browns Blue" livery, complete with authentic adverts and destination blinds and will play a major part in the Commemoration Weekend in March 2013. **Photo/ The Author**

CONTENTS

Mike Sutcliffe and Paul Banbury were given a vehicle destination board by the staff at Allen's of Mountsorrel upon their closure. Their only means of transport were their push bikes. They are seen here on a rather dangerous journey home. **Photo/ Maurice Darnes**

Acknowledgements

I would like to take this opportunity to thank the following people for their help over the past two years. I have visited many people, who for various reasons have had connections with Brown's Blue, family members, employees, passengers and enthusiasts. The response has been amazing, they have all been very helpful with information, photographs and ephemera.

John Arnold
Joe Bowley
Wynn and Norman Brown
Coalville Times
Betty Hill
Markfield Historical Society
The Omnibus Society
Ted and Mary Pepper
P.S.V. Circle
Malcolm Skerritt
Joan Bates
Alan Briggs
Lloyd and Pauline Burton
Clifford Hargrave
Bernard Hipwell
Jack Massey
Brian Partner
George Potter
Terry Riley
John White
Peter Blanchard
Wayne Brown
Michael Clark
Collin Harris
Ray Hurd
Audrey Morris
John Partner
Geoff Price
John Shilcott
Keith Wortley
Ray Morris M.I.R.T.E. M.S.O.E. A.M.I.M.I. Technical Engineer

Over the years many photographs have been taken by enthusiasts who have travelled many miles on all forms of transport including rail, bus, push bike and motor car. It goes without saying that without their dedication we would not be able to produce this book. I offer my sincere thanks to those listed below and offer my apologies to those I have missed!

1685 Group
Paul Banbury
John Botterill
John Clark Collection
Alan B. Cross
Michael Egan
Trevor Follows
W.J. Haynes
Leicester City Transport
G. Lumb
Geoff R. Mills
P.S.V. Circle
Arnold Richardson (Photobus)
Steve Sanders
Michael Sleath
T.G. Walker
S. N. J. White
John Allen
John Bennett
Richard Butler
C. J. Collin
Maurice Darnes
R. Ellis
Mike Greenwood
J. F. Higham
Leicester Mercury
Robert Mack
Peter Newland
R. B. Parr
C. W. Routh
SCT 61 Website
Mike Sutcliffe MBE
B. Weedon
Keith Wortley
Derek M. Bailey
A. Blackman
C. Carter
Allan T Condie
A. J. Douglas
East Pennine Transport Group
Robin N. Hannay
Ken Jubb
Leicestershire Records Office
Roy Marshall
Omnibus Society Collection
Bob Pearson
Julie Sanders
R.H.G. Simpson
Mark Swallow
Derek Westall
Peter Yeomans

Finally I would like to make special mention of the following people who have helped with content, planning and final design. It would not have been possible to complete this publication without their assistance.

Paul Banbury
John Bennett
Micheal Cockcroft
Allan T Condie
Andrew Gamble
Mike Greenwood
Ken Jubb
Peter Newland
Paul Odell

Please Note: Any photos credited to a 'collection' were not necessarily taken by the person named.

FOREWORD

BROWN'S BLUE

It will soon be fifty years since the last Brown's Blue bus departed from Marlborough Square in Coalville and the company and its vehicles seemed set to disappear from the west of Leicestershire and from people's memories.

Such was the influence of the business that Lawrence Brown set up in the 1920s that even today the mention of the name Brown's Blue brings forth a host of memories, passed down from grandparents and parents. There are the inevitable stories of the struggle to provide the bus service in winter weather, in thick fog and deep snow and these contrast with the recollections of happy days spent travelling to the seaside in summer for a few brief hours of relaxation and entertainment. In an era before almost universal car ownership the local bus company provided the link to the world beyond the village and was an integral part of daily life.

My own connection with Brown's Blue comes a little more recently. At a slide show in Leicester in the late1960s a picture was screened of two lines of double decker buses all in smart blue livery standing in the car park of the public house at Copt Oak. A few weeks later when purchasing petrol at Markfield I was surprised to see "Brown's Blue Garage" printed on the receipt. Shortly afterwards I located the former bus garages at Markfield (Flying Horse) and at Ibstock (Leicester Road and Melbourne Road), two of which still exist.

Mick Gamble has taken the research far beyond my preliminary enquiries, searching out members of the Brown family, many former employees, details of vehicles and routes and photographs until the point at which there seemed to be little left to discover. Then came the editing of all this information into the excellent publication for which I am privileged to write this forward. It is a worthy tribute to the Brown's Blue, ensuring that the memory of the company is secured for future generations to understand their history.

JOHN BENNETT
4th March 2012

Seen here in June 1980, the Author is taking a well earned break, after a stint at the wheel of the ex-Leicester Leyland PD3 82 HBC, which was purchased by Astill and Jordan Ltd of Ratby for its Leicester to Ratby service during 1978. One Man Operated vehicles used by Midland Red East under the "Lancer" banner were no match for the conductor operated vehicles of Astill and Jordan and Hylton and Dawson on the A50 (Groby Road). **Photo/ The Author**

Introduction

Brown's Blue, it rolls off of the tongue doesn't it. Almost fifty years have passed since one of Leicestershire's largest independent operators, Browns Blue, ceased its network of services in west Leicestershire, Friday 15th March 1963 was the final day of service; former London Transport double decker HLW 151 performed the last journey at 10.25 pm from Coalville (Marlborough Square) to Ibstock. Unfortunately I was not present at the time but I can imagine the deep sadness of those present and also that of the travelling public in the area, Services in west Leicestershire would never be quite the same again.

I have been fascinated by this particular bus company, for as long as I can remember. I can recollect, as a youngster seeing the vehicles passing through the Woodgate area in Leicester on my way to school. Woodgate is to this day a busy local shopping area to the west of Leicester city centre dissected by the main A50 trunk road. In those days traffic was very busy, this was the main route to the north west and there were many lorries and numerous bus services passing through the area, both local and longer distance. Services fed the industrial area of western Leicestershire as well as the beautiful Charnwood Forest. Fewer cars were on the road in those days and as a result of this bus services were well used.

Contrasts between the several different operators were always the focus of my attention, the bright red of the Midland Red vehicles contrasted strongly with the deep crimson and cream favoured by Leicester City Transport. Added to this were the various tones of blue and cream used by Astill and Jordan and the maroon and cream of Hylton and Dawson, both relatively small operators running less frequent services. The vehicles that caught my eye the most were those belonging to Browns Blue Coaches Ltd. who provided frequent services to and from west Leicestershire. The majority of vehicles, although not all, on stage carriage service were double deck finished in a deep blue and red colour scheme with gold script fleet names to finish off what was to my youthful eye, a very well presented group of vehicles. The double deck fleet always carried a wide range of colourful adverts, some local and some national.

Destination blinds offered travel to what I thought at the time were far off places such as Whitwick, Stanton-under-Bardon, Measham and Ashby de la Zouch. I now live in the area and they seem quite local.

West bound services left the city via Woodgate along the main A50 corridor towards Glenfield Turn; this was the area known as the Groby Road where competition between operators was most intense. During peak hours duplicates were often used inbound in the mornings and outbound in the evenings, buses would "leapfrog" the bus stops to maximise passenger loadings, this meant that the conductor needed to be "on the ball" with the bell.

I have worked in all aspects of the bus industry for nearly forty years and during the mid 1970's I was employed as a driver/manager for Astill and Jordan Ltd. For many years I gained valuable experience of the "competition" on the Groby Road. I also had the "doubtful honour" of driving the last half cab double deck bus in regular public service on the A50. As a point of interest, we were still using former Browns Blue Setright ticket machines!

Sadly all these memories are now in the past, but hopefully this insight into a company founded by Lawrence Daniel Brown, from humble beginnings, on January 1st 1924, will bring back many fond memories of personal service and reliability, unfortunately missing from some of today's multinational conglomerates. I have covered as much of the company's history as I can, without getting to 'bogged down' in statistics. Important national events have been included in the text at the appropriate times to help the reader to recognise the period in question. Vehicle details, acquisitions and withdrawals mentioned are as accurate as possible. Finally I have also tried to introduce the human element into the story; this is an important part of local history and without the management, staff and passengers there would be no need for a bus company.

It is inevitable that as soon as a manuscript goes for publication, further information comes to light, but I hope that after two years of research, this comprehensive and hopefully informative volume will give the reader as much enjoyment as it has me. I invite you to just sit back, relax and join me on a journey aboard **BROWN'S BLUE**.

HOLD TIGHT !

MICK GAMBLE

Formally Leicester City Transport No 270 JF 5873, Leyland TD3 with Metro-Cammell H26/24R bodywork dating from May 1934, is seen standing outside the Ibstock depot.
Photo/ 1685 Group R Hannay

Please note: Wherever the name Brown's Blue appears in the text with an apostrophe it refers to events before 1st July 1954 when L. D. Brown (Brown's Blue) became a limited company Browns Blue (Coaches) Ltd. All references made without the apostrophe refer to events after this date. (See chapter 6)

CHAPTER 1

THE NANCY

1st January 1924 to 31st December1929

There is little doubt that during the latter years of the First World War, workers in the coal mining industry were amongst the highest paid in the country. Dirty and often dangerous conditions, together with the long working hours were the main reasons for this.

After the Government took control of the Mining Industry in 1916 the threat of strikes was always a problem. In order to maintain constant production to meet wartime demands the Government met high wage increases with little resistance, thus feeding inflation which in turn increased the price of coal. Inevitably the 'bubble would burst' and in 1921 the price of coal at home and on the international markets collapsed, throwing the coal mining industry into turmoil. The mine owners would not pay the high wages that had previously been the norm, the miners became increasingly disenchanted with the situation, and constantly threatened strike action, this culminating in the General Strike of 1926.

Lawrence Daniel Brown
1901 - 1957

Lawrence Daniel Brown worked in the local coal mining industry at Bagworth Colliery and amidst all of the turmoil brought about by local disputes. His career came to an abrupt end in 1923 following a dispute with a pit superintendant over a colleague who was the victim of a bullying pit boss. Lawrence was a fair and honourable man and could not stand by without intervening. It was following this incident he considered that a life underground was not for him and he handed in his resignation and parted company with Bagworth Colliery. At the age of twenty two he started what was to become, the most successful private bus and coach business in Leicestershire.

Lawrence lived in Ashby Road, Markfield with his wife Thirza. They eventually had six children, three boys and three girls; the boys were Reginald, Norman and Terry, the girls were Dorrell, Enid and Betty. They all had a part to play within the company in future years although Dorell did train as a nurse in New Zealand for a few years before becoming a Sister at the Leicester Royal Infirmary.

Lawrence was a good friend of local haulier John (Jack) Hargrave who operated two small lorries. John dealt with Whitby's Garage in Narborough Road, Leicester and in 1923 he introduced Lawrence to the staff at Whitby's. Lawrence was keen to purchase his first vehicle, and with the help of John he arranged to purchase a small Chevrolet truck. It was agreed to part exchange his motorcycle and sidecar plus a small amount of cash as a deposit, the balance being made up with a loan secured by John.

They both rode the motorcycle combination into Leicester and Laurie was able to purchase his first vehicle which they drove back. It was a Chevrolet NR3541, a small lorry which could be fitted with a "Dixie" type 14 seat bus body which was very common in those days. The bus could be quickly transformed back into a small goods vehicle. Many small operators used this type of vehicle to maximise usage throughout the day.

Lawrence Brown proudly stands by his first acquisition a 1924 Chevrolet lorry NR 3541, which was fitted with a "Dixie" type 14 seat detachable bus body and named "The Nancy" after his younger sister. **Photo/ Leicester Mercury**

There were several other bus operators serving Markfield. Dick Warner established a service into Leicester ten years prior to Lawrence Brown's venture, the vehicles were garaged at The Green in Markfield village. Arthur Whetton ran daily services from Coalville to Leicester (his vehicle was affectionatly known as "The Ellen") and a man with a reputation for being a bit of a character. William Brown operated an unusual vehicle nicknamed "The Nippon", apparently not the most reliable of vehicles. Herbert Smith and Son operated from Stanton-u-Bardon into Leicester and to Loughborough, via Markfield, the subject of a takeover by Brown's a few years later.

On January 1st 1924 Lawrence Brown commenced operation with his "green" coloured Chevrolet from the premises in Ashby Road taking the work girls from Stanton-under-Bardon and Markfield to the shoe factories in nearby Anstey. After the morning run he would convert the bus into a small lorry, using it to deliver coal from the local pitheads to customers in the surrounding community. On her return from school in the afternoon, his younger sister Annie known as Nancy would clean off the coal dust and help convert the vehicle back into a bus in preparation for the return works journey which she conducted. Lawrence or Laurie as he was also known named the bus after his sister, and had the name painted on each side of the vehicle.

After many experiments with different colour schemes, he finally decided to adopt a deep blue and red livery and within a very short space of time the name of "Brown's Blue" became a well known local catchphrase.

It didn't take long for Laurie to repay his loan and in January 1925 a second Chevrolet NR 5701 was purchased again with a 14 seat body. In November of the same year a third Chevrolet NR 7669, possibly with 14 seat bodywork (although this has not been recorded) displaced the original Chevrolet which had started operations in 1924. By this time another driver was employed to assist with the extra work created both in the goods sector and also the expansion in the bus route network.

In March 1926 a Chevrolet X NR 8172 was purchased with 14 seat bodywork, followed a year later by a Dennis 30 cwt chassis UT 521 fitted with 18 seat coach bodywork. This replaced the second Chevrolet NR 5701, which was sold locally as a goods vehicle to Watson of Coalville. In May of the same year the Chevrolet X was withdrawn and sold, passing to Horton of Lutterworth. A Chevrolet LM UT 2055, with 14 seat bodywork was supplied new in February 1928, followed by the withdrawal of the Chevrolet R in July of that year and a month later a new Chevrolet LO UT 3563, again with 14 seat bodywork entered the fleet.

By this time expansion to the service network had taken place and buses were operating to the surrounding villages and further afield to Leicester and Whitwick. Tours, Excursions and Private Hire contracts were carried out using the Dennis coach. The haulage side of the business ran in parallel alongside the bus services during this time, although as a separate entity, this arrangement remained in place until the early war years.

A surprise purchase in April 1929 was that of a Renault R1 UL 2658 with 20 seat bodywork. This vehicle would serve the company for only a short time before its demise, following an unfortunate incident in 1930.

Laurie was extremely keen to expand his business. He successfully negotiated the purchase of local operator George E Hamblin of Groby on 3rd June 1929. Hamblin operated services from Groby to Leicester and these were integrated into Brown's growing route network. The single vehicle, a 14 seat Morris UT 694 was only kept for a short period and used for hire and was then sold in October 1929. During July the last Chevrolet, another LQ model UT5687, with 14 seat bodywork entered service, displacing the Chevrolet LM.

During the period from 1924 until 1930 Lawrence Brown turned what could have been a disastrous situation into a success story, during what were very difficult times. The next chapter will show how Laurie managed to sustain his business amidst strong competition from larger operators, followed by a period of expansion, including the opening of a new garage at Markfield.

During the Second World War and in the immediate post war period materials were in very short supply including paint. A variety of blues were used all basically similar, but not the same. The need to standardise on a specific colour was found to be necessary and with this in mind discussions were held with Duple Motor Bodies. A standard formulation was produced, not surprisingly it was labelled "Browns Blue". This was used alongside the red and in some cases primrose on all repaints involving coaches until late 1959, when a two-tone scheme was introduced using two lighter blues.

The double deck fleet was painted in mainly the deep blue livery, relieved by large areas of red in-between decks, the lower waistband band, wings and guard rails.

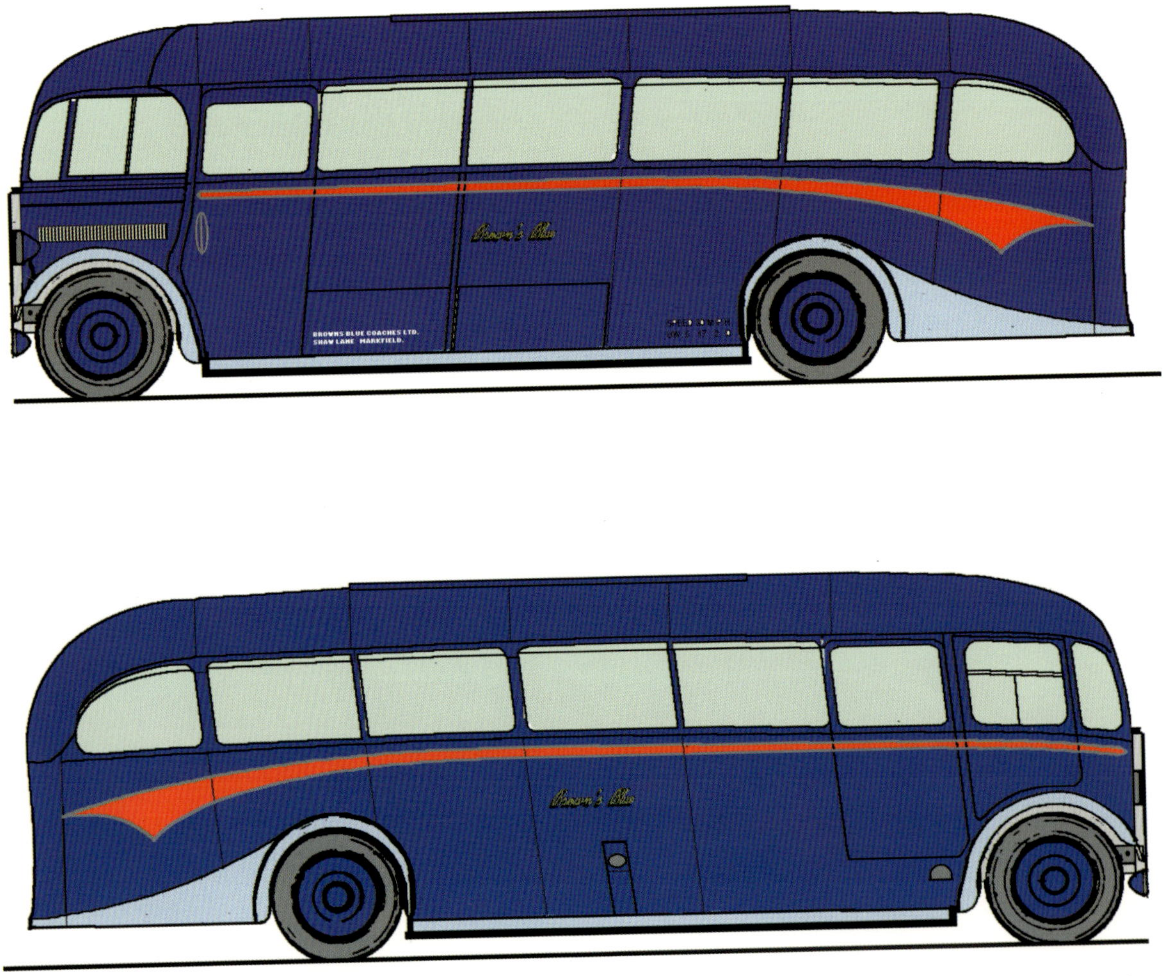

1950 Dennis Lancet III / Duple

From circa 1958 the amount of red was reduced to a strip above the lower deck windows, wings and guard rails. The exception to this was the Roberts bodied Daimler. It received two red bands when repainted, a scheme it retained until operations ceased in 1963.

However during the mid-fifties various temporary colour combinations were tried on a variety of vehicles, some were adopted but the majority were not. I am grateful to Transport Historian Allan T Condie, who has produced these detailed line drawings showing many of the various combinations tried.

1950 Leyland Comet / Burlingham

1948 AEC Regal 111 / Burlingham

1947 Dennis Lancet I I I / Yeates

1947 Leyland PS1 / Yeates

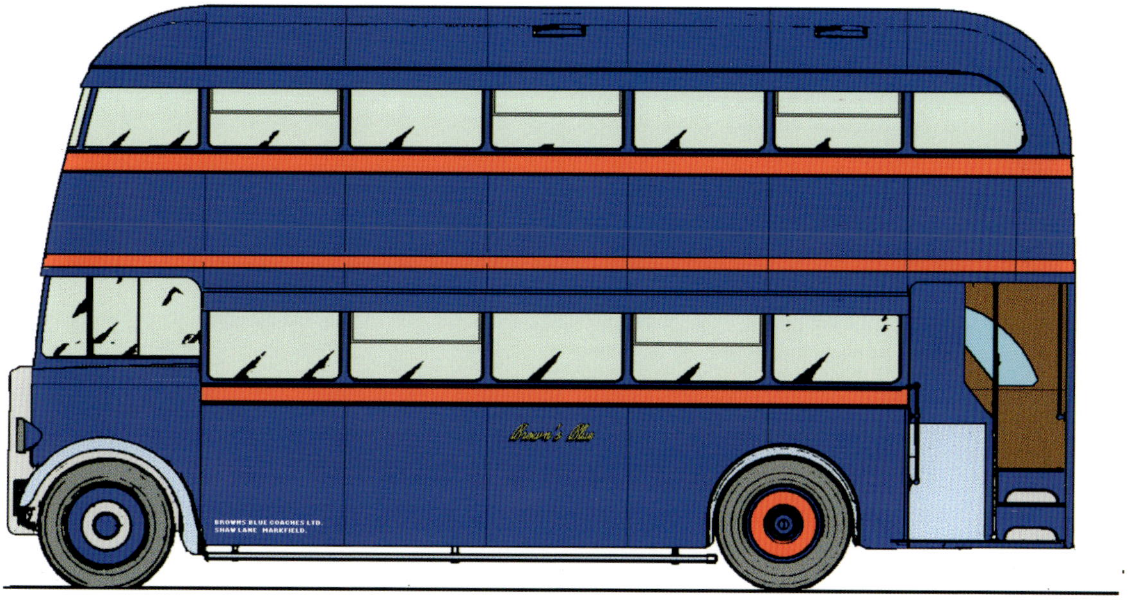

1951 Daimler CD650 / Roe

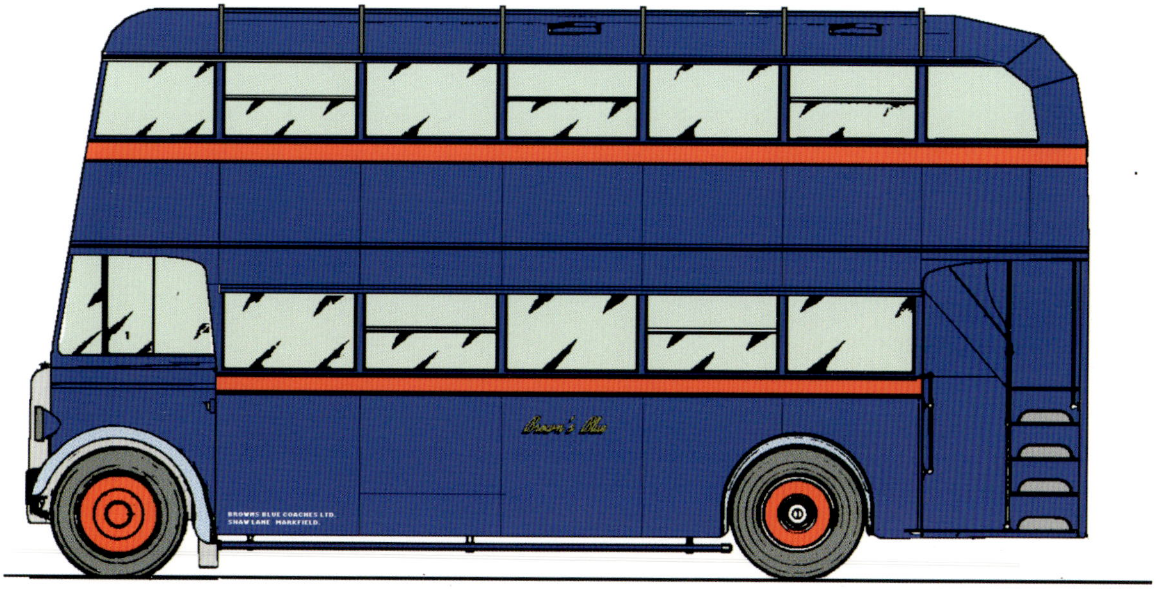

1944 Daimler CWA6 / Duple

1947 AEC RT / Park Royal or Weymann

1949 AEC Regent 111 / Weymann

1947 Daimler CVD6 / Brush

1949 Daimler CVD6 / Roberts

1947 Bedford OB / Duple

1948 Bedford OB / Yeates

All line drawings are reproduced with the kind permission of Allan T Condie.

CHAPTER II

PRE-WAR CONSOLIDATION

1st January1930 to 2nd September 1939

Moving into a new decade Laurie was determined to build upon his success in the last six years. However these were very difficult times for business expansion. The Great Depression had been felt as early as 1929 and lasted until the end of 1933.

A Labour government was returned to power in 1929 and was determined to push ahead with new policies. One piece of new legislation which would affect the bus and coach industry was The 1930 Road Traffic Act. These new regulations included a 30 mph speed limit for buses and coaches, the control of conduct of drivers, conductors and passengers on public service vehicles together with limitations on driving hours.

Unfortunatly, at this time Lawrence's brother Alfred was fatally injured in an accident involving one of Brown's vehicles, possibly one of the GMCs which overturned on a sharp bend outside Bardon Chapel. The family mourned the sad loss of "Uncle Alf" as he was fondly referred to, a memory still talked about by Norman Brown over eighty years later.

Laurie operated five vehicles, a Dennis coach, two Chevrolets, one GMC and a Renault which unfortunately caught fire on Nanpantan Hill when making a return journey from Loughborough market. The cause of this was found to be a leaking auto-vac system which was positioned above the exhaust manifold, fuel had dripped onto the red hot manifold and ignited. Fortunately there were no injuries and the vehicle was subsequently withdrawn from service and scrapped. In March 1930 a new twenty seat GMC T42 UT 6608 entered service. However the need for a larger capacity vehicles was becoming apparent and this would need to be addressed in the near future.

Following the acquisition of the business of George Hamblin in 1929, Laurie was keen to expand his route network. The competition between operators with these same ambitions was intense. The Midland Red had taken over many small independent operators throughout Leicestershire and was determined to gain a strong foothold in the county and beyond.

During the latter part of 1930, negotiations took place with Herbert Smith and Son (trading as Bertie Smith or Smith's) who operated from The Plough Inn, Stanton-under-Bardon. Subsequent success in the completion of the negotiations meant that the takeover was finalised on 1st January 1931. Two of the vehicles which were operated passed into Brown's fleet. These were both altered for use as goods vehicles, the remainder were withdrawn and sold. Smith's stage carriage services between Stanton and Leicester (All Saints Road), were integrated into Brown's timetables, thus consolidating routes from Stanton to Leicester, Loughborough, Whitwick and Coalville.

Applications for stage carriage services were submitted to the Traffic Commissioners during the early part of 1931 and heard at the County Court, Leicester on 15th June 1931. They consisted of four applications and were as follows:-

Markfield and **Loughborough** via Shaw Lane, Copt Oak, Woodhouse Lane and Charley Cross Roads. **GRANTED**

Leicester and **Whitwick** via Groby, Markfield, Greenhill and Forest Rock.

(Hitherto to be Sunday, Wednesday and Saturday, but to be daily) **GRANTED** Sunday, Wednesday and Saturday only.

Leicester and **Stanton under Bardon** via Groby, Markfield and Shaw Lane. **GRANTED**

Stanton under Bardon and **Coalville** via Shaw Lane, and Bardon Hill. **GRANTED**

Further applications were made in July/August and were heard at the Crown Court, Leicester on 9th November 1931. They consisted of two applications and were as follows:-

Markfield and **Desford Colliery** via Shaw Lane, Stanton, Ellistown Colliery and Bagworth. **GRANTED**

Stanton under Bardon and **Anstey** via Shaw Lane Markfield and Newtown Linford. **GRANTED**

More applications were made in late August/early September and were also heard at Leicester Crown Court on 9th November 1931. They consisted of two applications and were as follows:-

Excursions and tours from Markfield. **GRANTED**

Excursions and tours from Humberstone Gate, Leicester. **WITHDRAWN**

Finally one application was made during October and was heard at the Grand Jury Room, Guildhall, Nottingham on 2nd December 1931

All of these applications were made under the "E" series of numbers.

Annual renewals of licences were made in 1932 and were numbered sequentially in the TER series. TER 79 was L. D. Brown, Markfield.

Existing licences were renewed with some alterations and additions as follows:-

Leicester and **Stanton under Bardon** via Groby, Markfield and Shaw Lane (altered to be Cliffe Lane not Shaw Lane).

Excursions and tours from Humberstone Gate, Leicester. (re-application).

Markfield and **Coalville** via Shaw Lane, Bardon Chapel and Birchtree. (exchange of tickets with W. D. Warner and W. Parsons).

Copt Oak and **All Saints Road, Leicester** via Ulvescroft, Markfield and Groby (Friday only).

Markfield and **Leicester City Football Ground Filbert Street** via Groby, Glenfield Turn, Fosse Road and Upperton Road. (August to May home matches).

Delivered in August 1934, Dennis Lancet JU 4723 with luxurious Willowbrook 32 seat coachwork remained with the company until November 1945 when it was sold to Applewhite, Dunham-on-Trent. **Photo/ Willowbrook**

To cope with the further increase in passenger traffic, Brown's first "heavyweight" chassis was purchased from Willowbrook stock in January 1931, this was a Maudslay ML3BC with Willowbrook 32 seat bodywork UT 8193 and also a Commer Invader with Willowbrook 20 seat bodywork UT 8355, which was placed into service at the same time. In October the first of many Bedfords arrived, this was a WLB model UT 9568, also seating 20. Finally a Lancia VF 1551, was purchased at about this time but very little is known about this vehicle. Withdrawals during 1931 consisted of the Renault R1 UL 2658 during May and one of the Chevrolet LQs UT 5687 in November.

1932 brought a single second-hand purchase in the form of a 26 seat GMC UT 3163, which entered service via Leicestershire operator, Peberdy of Fleckney. Withdrawal of the last of the low capacity vehicles placed into service in the late twenties took place in this year, the Dennis coach UT 521 was taken out of service in June and altered for use as a goods vehicle and the last of the Chevrolets, an LO model UT 3563, was de-licensed in September.

Very little changed in the fleet during 1933 as efforts were concentrated on maintaining and improving services and expanding into private hire and coach operation. A second Bedford WLB JU 2562, with 20 seat bodywork was purchased in September, this was the last 20 seat vehicle to be purchased.

The beginning of Brown's Blue's long association with the Dennis heavyweight chassis started during 1934 when in August of that year a Dennis Lancet with Willowbrook 32 seat bodywork JU 4723

Taken at the Willowbrook works this official photograph shows the 1935 Bedford WTL 25 seat coach JU 6301, fitted with service type doors. **Photo/ Willowbrook**

was delivered. The Lancia VF 1551, was withdrawn at this time and sold to Matthews of Shouldham.

In February 1935 another vehicle to pass to Matthews of Shouldham was the GMC UT 3163 purchased in 1932, at the same time the first Bedford WLB UT 9568 passed to Wordsall, Earith. During May a Bedford WTL JU 6301, with stylish coachwork by Willowbrook entered service. It was suitable for bus or coach duties and featured comfortable seats, curtains, a roof rack and sliding roof. It was fitted with "bus type" folding doors, obviously Lawrence Brown had an eye on dual purpose use. At this time fleet strength stood at six buses plus several lorries which were used for coal deliveries and local quarry work.

So to 1936, midway through the decade, the abdication year of Edward V111. Also at this time 'storm clouds' were gathering in Europe. Adolf Hitler's domination of power both in Germany and many neighbouring countries was the cause of a great deal of concern to the British Government. However the British public were still enjoying the benefits of a reasonable standard of living. Entertainment was of major importance, people needed to take their minds off of the impending doom and gloom which was about to throw the world into disarray for most of the next decade. Dance Halls and Movie Theatres were popular, most large villages and towns had at least one Movie Theatre, commonly known in the Midlands area as the "Pictures or Flicks". Thousands would flock to see their movie favourites, such as James Stewert, Micky Rooney, Carol Lombard, Clark Gable and many more! Most people needed transport, very few had their own cars. The

The driveway at Markfield (Shaw Lane) garage is the location for this lineup of Brown's coaches plus one Vauxhall taxi, Driver Eric Partner stands by the 1937 Bedford WTB AJU 230 with Duple C25F coachwork. Photo/ Eric Partner

buses were busy and duplicating the last bus of the evening was a regular occurance.

Most commodities and goods were in relatively plentiful supply, town centres were busy, market days were popular and extra services were always run on these days to meet demand. Each town had its own market day which allowed bus operators to work their timetables accordingly. Lawrence Brown was well aware of this and adjusted services to suit. On 1st January a new timetable was introduced between Leicester (All Saints' Road) and Whitwick (Market Place). Services ran on Sundays (six journeys), Wednesdays (six journeys plus two in the evening Whitwick to Leicester only) and Saturdays (eight journeys plus two in the evening Whitwick to Leicester only). A Saturday service was operated on Bank Holiday Mondays and Tuesdays.

Larger vehicles were needed to meet the demand and an increase in fleet size was also a possibility. During July 1936 Lawrence Brown's "love affair" with AEC buses began, an AEC Regal JU 9148 with Burlingham 32 seat bodywork entered service.

In 1937, the Coronation year, George VI was crowned King on 12th May. Celebrations were held in the newly opened garage yard at Shaw Lane, Markfield and members of the local community were invited to take part in what was a very joyous occasion. In May of this year a new Bedford WTB AJU 230, with Duple 25 seat entered service and in the following month another AEC Regal AJU 358, this time with Mulliner (Northampton) 32 seat bodywork was purchased. This was a very imposing vehicle, far more luxurious than anything operated before, but would sadly only serve in the fleet for a very short period.

Both AECs were taken by the War Department in 1939. Another withdrawal in 1937 was the last of the twenties style 20 seat normal control vehicles, a GMC T42 UT 6608.

Delivered during July 1936, AEC Regal JU 9148 with Burlingham C32R bodywork is taken in December 1951 at Hertford Station, working for Hertfordshire Agricultural Executive (C'TEG). Unfortunately this vehicle never returned to Brown's Blue. Photo/ Alan B Cross

AJU 358 was the second AEC Regal purchased before the war; this vehicle carried Mulliner (Northampton) 32 seat coachwork. Both of the AEC Regal's were requisitioned by the military. Photo/ Mulliner

A second Bedford WTB BAY 18, entered service in June 1938, this was also bodied by Duple but had seating for 26. At this time a second hand Bedford WTB ARW 864 was purchased with Duple 25 seat bodywork, from Bunty Motorways of Coventry.

As the probability of war with Germany increased, many smaller companies had what can only be described as "flagship vehicles" requisitioned by the War Department; these were then allocated to the forces for troop movements. Some vehicles entered service with the British Armed Forces and later with the U.S. military, inevitably very few were returned to their original owners.

Therefore both of the AEC Regals were requisitioned during 1939 leaving a shortage of vehicles in the fleet. To compensate this, Brown's Blue turned to second hand purchases, two Dennis Lancet IIs ANR 216 and AUE 27 both with Willowbrook 32 seat bodywork were joined by another Bedford WTB BJU 779 with Duple 26 seat bodywork, purchased in March 1939 locally from Philips, of Enderby.

Apart from the impending deterioration in world affairs, another significant event took place during 1939 which would have a major affect upon Brown's Blue services.

St. Margaret's Bus Station was opened, replacing the crowded "street stands" that had been in place since the 1920s. All Saints Road which still runs directly under the Great Central Railway Station (now an industrial estate) was the site of a bus station, which at best was totally inadequate for its purpose. All county services entering

Purchased as replacements for the AECs were two second hand Dennis Lancet I Is. ANR 216 with Willowbrook bodywork from local operator Toone, of Billesdon. The vehicle at the rear is Leyland Tiger BNR 59 carrying its original Plaxton bodywork. **Photo/ Alan B Cross**

the city from the west terminated at this point leaving passengers quite a lengthy walk to the city centre. The new centrally placed bus station would serve a far wider area covering west, north and east Leicestershire. However passengers travelling from the south-west, south and south-east would still terminate their journeys at Western Boulevard, The Newark and Northampton Square, respectively all a lengthy walk from town. These arrangements remained in place until the mid-sixties. This was part of the area bus stop system put in place by the Leicester Corporation Tramways Department.

On the eve of the outbreak of war 2nd September 1939, the company fleet strength stood at ten vehicles, one Maudslay, six Bedfords and three Dennis.

The people of Great Britain would wake up to a very different world on the morning of 3rd September 1939. How would this affect Brown's Blue and its services? We will take a look at this in Chapter Three.

The second replacement came from Edwards of Bishops Itchington, AUE 27 was a similar vehicle and is pictured here at Ibstock depot in 1954. **Photo/ R F Mack**

Chapter III

Wartime Austerity

September 1939 To December 1945

The outbreak of World War Two had a profound effect on the area. The numerous coal mines in the area were put under more and more pressure to increase production. Industry was working flat out to meet the demand to service the war effort, this had repercussions on the local labour market. Conscription had taken its toll and the majority of available manpower was being absorbed by the collieries.

Many bus companies in the area struggled to maintain an adequate number of employees to fulfil their service commitments and most private hire and excursions had by this time ceased. Companies concentrated on Stage Carriage Services and Works Contracts. Drivers and conductors often worked long hours to make up the shortfall. Women were also trained to carry out both types of duty. With the onset of fuel rationing timetables were adjusted accordingly with non-essential journeys being discontinued and extra works services introduced to meet demand. This was offset to a certain degree by increased mileage incurred through the high demand for troop movements.

The War Department was responsible for the allocation of all new and second hand vehicles and through the Ministry of Supply they assessed the needs of each operator. Second hand withdrawals and purchases were also monitored by the ministry as were the use of new and second hand spare parts. These all could be obtained from the numerous Government compounds scattered throughout the country.

Guy and Daimler were responsible for new heavy weight chassis production, the majority of which were fitted with double deck bodies. AEC, Leyland and Bristol were allowed to supply "Unfrozen" chassis on a reduced basis, but this was only while existing pre-war stocks lasted. Lightweight single deck chassis were supplied by Bedford who introduced the OWB especially for the purpose. Bodywork was built by several different manufacturers, but were all designed to "Utility" specification minimising and conserving the use of materials which were in short supply. Some body builders had large stocks of pre-war materials available and were allowed to use these up to meet demand. Some of these vehicles although classed as utility, were in fact built to a very relaxed specification, but as these stocks were used up most vehicles appeared with the square, angular appearance associated with the utility design.

It was essential if Lawrence's two older sons Reg and Norman were to be involved in the future running of the business that they gain experience in commercial vehicle maintenance and operation. Lawrence Brown had built up a strong relationship with local commercial vehicle suppliers and repairers Ford and Slater of Leicester,

One of four Bedford OWB Utilities supplied new to Brown's Blue during the war, CUT 345 is seen here standing outside St. Margaret's Bus Station in the immediate post war period. This vehicle carried Duple bodywork when new, but in common with the other Bedford's in the fleet was down seated during 1947/48. **Photo/ Alan B Cross**

Unfortunately there are no photographs of the 1936 AEC Regal VD 6508 with Pickering C32F bodywork purchased by Brown's Blue via the Ministry allocation system during 1940; however this photograph shows a similar vehicle VD 6510 from the same batch working for J. J. Baker in County Durham. **Photo/ Roy Marshall**

A second hand acquisition during 1940 was that of a 1939 AEC Regal BDB 385 with Burlingham coachwork, it was probably purchased through the War Department. **Photo/ W J Haynes / A. P. Newland Collection**

CUT345 taken in later years after withdrawal in July 1950, it was purchased for non-psv use in the London area. **Photo/ R F Mack**

It is thought that this photo was taken on 27th July 1947. The location is Melton Turn, Leicester. The tram network in Leicester was finally abandoned in November 1949, in favour of a large replacement program involving one hundred and sixty new double deck buses. Our focus is drawn to the Bedford Utility bus on the left owned by Brown's Blue, far away from its normal stage carriage operating area It is possibly working a works contract. It is worth noting the Leyland Tiger coach just peeping out from behind the tram, it is a Harrington bodied coach belonging to Southdown Motor Services, also far away from its normal operating area. **Photo/ R.B. Parr A.P. Newland Collection**

mainly through the supply of several new Vulcan Tipper Lorries for the haulage side of the business, Lawrence arranged with the company for his sons to enter employment upon leaving school, firstly Reg Brown joined Ford and Slaters as an apprentice mechanic, followed by his younger brother Norman. However conscription prematurely ended their careers, although these were subsequently continued during their wartime service with the R.E.M.E.

During 1940 three second hand AEC Regal coaches were purchased via the War Department VD 6508 carried Pickering bodywork, BDB 385 was bodied by Burlingham and HRF 102 was purchased in March 1940 carrying Harrington bodywork. However this was returned to the WD during July 1940.

Withdrawal of the Maudsley UT 8193, took place in January 1942 and was sold through the Ministry to Fieldsend, of Salford, Lancs.

The lorry fleet had been kept busy during the early war years, delivering coal and quarry products to the various factories and construction sites throughout the Midlands which were committed to the war effort. After the disastrous bombing of Coventry on the night of 14th November 1940, Brown's lorries were sent to Coventry to assist with the massive clear up effort needed to return the city to some sought of normality.

It was in 1942 that Lawrence Brown decided to close down the haulage part of the business, allowing him to concentrate on the buses. This had run in parallel with the buses since the company started in 1924 and a total of six lorries were operated. These and the "O" licences were sold locally to the Cliffe Hill Granite Company.

The sale of the haulage business allowed for the expansion of the bus fleet. In September 1942 Browns received their first new utility vehicle allocated by the Ministry of Supply. This was a Bedford OWB CNR 224 fitted with Roe 32 seat bodywork, and this was followed in February 1943 by a similar vehicle CNR 436. In April 1944 two further Bedford OWB utilities CUT 344 and CUT 345, this time with Duple 32 seat bodywork were delivered.

Finally another withdrawal overseen by the Ministry was that of the second Bedford WLB JU 2562 this vehicle passed to Barker, Mablethorpe.

The war in Europe was drawing to a close by 1945 but wartime restrictions were still in place. Two further withdrawals overseen by the Ministry took place during 1945, firstly in March the Bedford WTL JU 6301 placed in service in May 1935 was sold to Thomas, North Muskham and in November the first Dennis Lancet to be withdrawn, JU 4723, purchased new in 1934, passed to Applewhite, Dunham-on-Trent.

Almost seven years of immense hardship and sadness were now drawing to a close, the post-war period was about to throw up fresh challenges, the inevitable increases in stage carriage service, vehicle replacement, the introduction of double deck operation and the continuing expansion brought about by the purchase of other operators within the area would all have a significant affect upon the future of Brown's Blue.

CHAPTER IV

POST WAR BOOM

January 1946 To January 1951

Although the Second World War had officially ended on 2nd September 1945 serious shortages of most commodities would be experienced for many years to come In fact to cope with these difficulties the Government continued rationing and in some cases decreased allowances. This policy would be in place for a further nine years making life difficult for a population that had already suffered many years of hardship and anxiety during the war.

In common with all other bus and coach operators maintaining Brown's Blue services had been very difficult. Staff shortages due to conscription and better rates of pay elsewhere in the local coal mining industry, had been overcome by employing staff of more senior years and also training women as platform staff. Vehicle maintenance was carried out as much as circumstances would allow, but shortages of spare mechanical parts meant that repairs were often short term in nature with second hand parts being reconditioned and fitted just to keep vehicles mobile. In some cases new parts were manufactured in the workshops.

Bodywork had suffered through the lack of maintenance brought about by material shortages and the enforced use of unsuitable materials such as unseasoned wood. Supplies of all metals and paint were also affected. Inevitably some vehicles began to look a little tired, but the garage staff had done their best to keep the wheels turning against the odds and fleet strength stood at about ten vehicles in December 1945, eight Bedfords, two AECs and one Dennis.

The Ministry of Supply and the Ministry of War Transport were still responsible for allocating new and second hand vehicles to operators. This was dependent upon their need and was strictly assessed by the Ministry. Major repairs and vehicles withdrawn and sold were also treated in the same manner, operators who did not qualify for new vehicles were permitted to purchase second hand vehicles from the Ministry storage compounds around the country. This system would be in place until 1946 and to a lesser degree beyond. In January of that year the Bedford WTB BJU 779 which was purchased in March 1939 was sold to King of the Road, Worthing.

At this time a significant change in both fleet strength and service commitments would have a major impact on the future of the company, making it well placed to take advantage of the impending boom in public transport usage.

During June 1946 the business of Albert Richard Hipwell was taken over. Trading as Green Bus Service and based at the Green Bus Service Garage, 41, Leicester Road, Ibstock, it became Browns main base in Ibstock. Eleven vehicles in total were absorbed into the Brown's fleet, doubling

This former Hipwell 1937 Bedford WTB AAY 679 with Duple bodywork stands outside the Ibstock depot in July 1950. It had been recently repainted into Brown's livery, however it would not be long before it would move to Ward of Oakham in May 1952. **Photo/ Robin Hannay**

fleet strength overnight. Vehicles involved in the transfer were as follows, two REO PullmansUT 5848 and UT 6207, dating from 1929, five Dennis Lancets JU 698, JU 3054, JU 7225, RC 1525 and AAY 6, all with Willowbrook bodywork and four Bedfords, two WTBs AAY 679 and AUT 287 and two Bedford OWBs CUT 343 and DAY 146.

Several services were taken over including Ibstock to Coalville, Ibstock to Ashby,

Taken during the nineteen thirties this photograph shows Hipwells No 2 a 1929 Reo Pullman registration number UT 6207 with Bracebridge 26 seat bodywork. The driver Len Briers and the vehicle both joined Brown's Blue in June 1946, the Reo was withdrawn in 1948.
Photo/ Julie Sanders

Coalville to Hinckley and local colliery services, some excursion and tour licences were also acquired.

A major change in Brown's Blue vehicle policy took place in August 1946 when the first double deck bus entered the fleet in the form of a 1931 Leyland Titan TD1 ED 6463, with Massey 54 seat bodywork which came originally from Warrington Corporation. This was also the first Leyland to enter the fleet. The increased capacity of this vehicle proved to be extremely useful on the busier sections of the route network such as the Ibstock to Coalville service and Leicester to Whitwick.

Passengers travelling on a sunny clear day by double decker on the Whitwick service at Irish Hill, were for the first time, treated to panoramic views of north-east Leicestershire stretching from Charnwood Forest in the foreground over Loughborough to the Vale of Belvoir in the distance. If they were quick and looked in

Former Hipwell a 1935 Dennis lancet JU 7225 with Willowbrook bodywork stands outside the depot in Leicester Road, Ibstock. **Photo/ Roy Marshall**

A dull dreary day in St. Margaret's Bus Station, former Hipwell Dennis Lancet delivered in 1933 originally carried Willowbrook bodywork; it is seen here after receiving the Harrington 32 seat body from former Warners Leyland Tiger TS2 FV 1550 during 1952. **Photo/ Omnibis Society Collection**

Photographed when new Hipwells AAY 6 a 1936 Dennis Lancet carries a 39 Willowbrook coach body. This vehicle entered the Brown's fleet in June 1946. It was fitted with an AEC 7.7 oil engine and re-bodied by Yeates in 1955. The new body seated 37 and was built to a fully fronted design. **Photo/ Omnibus Society Collection**

the opposite direction they would catch views of south-west Leicestershire stretching over to south Staffordshire and beyond to the Wenlock Edge near the Welsh border.

Taking advantage of some layover time, the crew of former Hipwell Bedford OWB DAY 146 delivered in September 1945 with Duple bus bodywork, is parked at the rear of the bays in St. Margaret's. Vehicles normally pulled to the front of the stand ten minutes before departure time. **Photo/ Roy Marshall**

In October of the same year two second hand Bedford OWBs with consecutive DWD 795 and DWD 796, and with Duple bodywork were purchased from Lloyds of Nuneaton. Seating was altered to 28 before entering service. However repainting was kept to a minimum, a red band below the windows and red mudguards were added to the original dark blue and cream livery used by Lloyds.

The success of the first Leyland double decker encouraged Brown's to purchase two more similar vehicles ED 6464 and ED 6560, from the same source. The first of these was identical to the previous purchase, but in January 1947 a similar vehicle arrived, this time with Brush bodywork. These vehicles were still fitted with petrol engines but Brown's carried out the "Covrad" conversions before they entered service, replacing the older design of Leyland radiator with a more modern full length version. A surprising addition to the fleet during February 1947 was the return of AEC Regal HRF 102.

L.D. Brown also ran some taxis from Markfield. Two large Vauxhall limousines were used for a variety of purposes including private hire, weddings, and the occasional funeral, usually on hire to the Co-operative Funeral Service. These vehicles were fitted with powerful six cylinder petrol engines. One was later fitted with a Perkins P6 diesel engine in the interests of fuel economy. This was not a complete success and after a short period the original engine was reinstated. In later years the taxi fleet was supplemented by a Humber Pullman.

Wartime restrictions concerning the manufacture and supply of new buses were now being relaxed and L.D. Brown was able to place orders for new vehicles with a variety of manufacturers. In March 1947 a new AEC Regal DUT 554, with Duple 35 seat bodywork.

A month later a Dennis Lancet VI EAY 58, with Yeates 35 seat bodywork was delivered. This became the first vehicle to complete its service life to the final day of operation with Browns Blue in March 1963, albeit in re-bodied form. A second Dennis Lancet III EJU 260, also with Yeates 35 seat bodywork, entered service in September and also remained in service in re-bodied form until March 1963.

Three former Warrington Corporation Leyland TD1s were the first double deck vehicles to enter the fleet in 1946/47. ED 6464 carries Massey 54 seat bodywork. All three vehicles were fitted with a "Covrad" radiator conversion before entering service. **Photo/ J F Higham**

Delivered in March 1947, AEC Regal DUT 554 with Duple coach bodywork was the first new vehicle delivered after the end of the Second World War. This rear view was taken in Marlborough Square, Coalville, and shows the original company details used during the immediate post war period. **Photo/ Omnibus Society Collection**

Another view of AEC Regal DUT 554 taken in St. Margaret's Bus Station, Leicester. **Photo/ A. P. Newland Collection**

Dennis Lancet III EAY 58 with 35 seat Yeates coachwork was the second new vehicle delivered in April 1947, it was rebodied during January 1960 using the Yeates body from AAY 6. **Photo/ Unknown**

1939 AEC Regal HRF 102 was originally purchased in March 1940 before being requisitioned by the WD in July 1940, it was returned to Brown's Blue in February 1947. It carried stylish Harrington bodywork which seated 32 passengers and was nicknamed "The Ducktail" because of its rather bulbous rear end. During 1953 the body was removed and the chassis fitted with an AEC 7.7 oil engine, the chassis was lengthened and dispatched to Yeates in Loughborough, where a new fully fronted coach body was fitted. **Photo/ W J Haynes / A P Newland Collection**

Making its way towards Copt Oak Dennis Lancet III EJU 260 with Yeates bodywork was delivered new in October 1947. It later received the fully fronted body from Dennis rebuild JU 7854 in February 1960. Photo/ R. F. Mack

Possibly one of the most significant signs of the company's success was the delivery in December 1947 of the first new double decker. A Daimler CVD6 chassis was chosen, with bodywork built by Brush. With 30 seats upstairs and 26 down. The interior was very well appointed with varnished wood mouldings and ornate opaque glass light fittings. Registered EJU 541 it was similar to Daimlers delivered to Derby Corporation at about the same time and was probably added to an existing order, a common practice by bodybuilders when building a single vehicle for a smaller operator.

The livery used on the double deckers at this time favoured large areas of red with blue relief. The blue used was specially formulated and mixed by Duple Motor Bodies and known as "Browns Blue"; the red used was a standard Post Office Red. This would change over the years, with more emphasis on blue. "Browns Blue" was written in large gold script below the lower deck windows. This did not last and it had been painted over by the time the platform doors had been fitted in 1952. A smaller gold script name was placed in a central position below the lower deck windows.

The driving staff would need to master the idiosyncrasies of the Wilson Pre-Selector gearbox, an easier option than the more normal "crash" gearbox they had been used to.

On the one occasion I had a drive in such a vehicle the owner said, and I quote, "It's like owning a dog, you need to establish who's boss. Show any signs of weakness or in this case lack of concentration and it will bite you in the shins!" Basically when the gear was selected and the gear change pedal operated a positive and direct stamp on the pedal was needed, "pussyfoot" around and the pedal would shoot out further than

The first new double deck vehicle to be purchased entered the fleet in January 1948, EJU 541 was a Daimler CVD6 with Brush bodywork, it was added to an existing order for Derby Corporation and was built to their specification, a common practice during this period when independent operators were placing single orders. **Photo/ A. P. Newland Collection**

normal and crack your shin. Further to this it would need two feet plus lots of pressure and leverage pressing against the seat backrest to return the pedal to its normal position. Needless to say drivers soon learned to handle these vehicles.

The wartime Bedford saloons had been delivered to 32 seat specification with slatted wooden seating. It was decided to fit upholstered seating at this time, a slight reduction in seating capacity resulted with a new specification of 28 seats.

In January 1948 the business of W.D. Warner and Sons, of Main Street, Markfield was acquired. This included six stage carriage services, excursion and tour licences, plus a total of ten vehicles. The purchase consolidated services between Markfield and Leicester. A Thursday only service from Markfield to Loughborough and a Sunday evening circular service leaving Markfield at 6.00p.m., in a clockwise direction and serving Newtown Linford, Anstey, Glenfield, Kirby Muxloe, Ratby, Groby and Markfield, returning by the reverse route at 10.00p.m. were also included. This was known locally as the "Picture Bus", serving the small cinema in Ratby and the various village pubs were the destination of the users of this popular service.

Vehicles included in the sale were as follows:- two Leyland Tiger TS1s WW 6814 and DK 7378 respectively, and one Leyland TS2 FV 1550, the chassis of which was later scrapped and the body fitted to one of the ex-Hipwell Dennis Lancets, two Dennis Lancet IIs JU 7854 and DRF 530, one Maudsley SF40 with Burlingham bodywork,

Taken in St. Margaret's Bus Station whilst still in the ownership of W. D. Warner this 1931 Leyland Tiger TS2 FV 1550 with Harrington C32F bodywork passed into the Brown fleet in January 1948. After suffering accident damage during 1952 the body was removed and fitted to Dennis Lancet JU 3054, the chassis was scrapped (see page 29 lower).
Photo/ Omnibus Society Collection

TH 7165, one Bedford WTB AUT 694, one Leyland Lion LT8 GLL 939, and two Bedford OWBs CNR 362 and CNR 480. This now bought the total of Bedford OWBs in the fleet to nine. Former Lloyd of Nuneaton Bedford OWB DWD 796 was sold at this time to Millbrook Steamboat and Trading Company Ltd a bus and boat operator from the River Tamar area.

Supplied new in January 1948, Bedford OB EJU 786 with Yeates bodywork stands in St. Margaret's Bus Station, Leicester. **Photo/ Roy Marshall**

A new Bedford OB EJU 786, with Yeates 29 seat bodywork was delivered at the same time.

Although the War Department compounds were a useful source for second hand vehicles, there were also many useful spare parts available. Lawrence Brown decided to purchase a number of spare engines of both AEC and Dennis manufacture from local dealer Murphy Brothers who had several sites in the Leicester area. These proved invaluable during the mid-fifties when several coach rebuilds took place, some double deckers also gained a new lease of life as a result of an engine change. At this time a new bus washing system was installed at Shaw Lane Garage, a far cry from the old "bucket, brush and hosepipe" method.

Delivered in June 1948 Tilling Stevens ENR 792 is seen here in St. Margaret's Bus Station on 28th September 1956, the rare Theale bodywork fits uneasy on the Tilling Stevens chassis, giving the impression of being built in two halves, in some ways the rear section resembles Duple design. **Photo/ Richard Butler**

Lawrence Brown could never be accused of being dull in his vehicle purchasing policy! Three rare Tilling Stevens K6LA7's ENR 792, EUT 52 and EUT 947, with equally rare Theale C32F bodywork entered service in June. Unfortunately poor paintwork preparation resulted in paint peeling off the bodywork and the three vehicles were sent back to the coachbuilders for repainting.

These vehicles were never very popular with the drivers, they were considered to be slow and ponderous in service and not the ideal vehicle for longer distance travel, where a top speed of only 38 m.p.h. was achieved. In later years the condition of the bodywork structure left much to be desired and not surprisingly these were amongst the first of the post-war deliveries to be withdrawn. To make way for these latest acquisitions the AEC Regal VD 6508 supplied in 1940, the first of the Bedford OWBs CNR 224 and the second former Hipwell REO UT 5848 were withdrawn. Another former Hipwell vehicle sold at this time was the oldest of the Dennis Lancet's JU 698. Two former Warner vehicles also failed to escape the onslaught; after only a few months under Brown's ownership the Bedford WTB AUT 694, passed to local operator Howlett`s of Quorn, and the Maudsley SF40 TH 7165 moved locally in the opposite direction to Gibson of Barlestone, ironically returning to Gibson's eight years after being sold by them to Warners. Exactly one year after taking delivery of their first new double decker, a second Daimler vehicle was purchased FAY 517, again with Brush bodywork, this time added to an order for ten similar vehicles for Exeter Corporation.

One of three similar vehicles this Tilling Stevens K6LA7 EUT 947 carried rare Theale bodywork;. It is pictured here in St. Margaret's Bus Station, Leicester, when almost new. **Photo/ Alan B Cross**

Fleet numbering had not been taken too seriously; staff preferred referring to the vehicles by their number plates. A system was introduced at about this time and loosely adhered to for a couple of years, but the number plate system remained in place throughout.

As 1948 drew to a close the expected boom in passenger numbers had established itself. During the previous two years many ex-servicemen had returned to the area, seeking employment in local collieries, many factories were setting on extra staff to cope with the industrial demand needed to put the country back on its feet. Workers contract services remained an important part of Brown's operations. These were austere times, but people were used to making a little go a long way. Rationing was still a big part of everyday life, but journeys to the shops in the local towns, especially on market days were slowly increasing and visits to the cinema, dance halls and the numerous working men's clubs in the area were beginning to have an effect on passenger loadings in the evenings and at weekends. In response to this higher demand timetables were adjusted and vehicle purchasing policy was reviewed, 1949 would possibly be the most important year in the company's history so far.

I think now is the best time to explain the "Area stop sign" system put in place by Leicester Corporation Tramways during the 1920s. All main trunk roads entering the city were served by the tramway system and in order to protect these services the "Area stop sign" system was introduced. The tram stops and in later years the bus stops adjacent to the city boundary were painted

The second new Daimler double decker FAY 517 was delivered in December 1948, it was again fitted with Brush 56 seat bodywork but this time added to an order for Exeter Corporation. The stylish but typically period fleet name written on each side of the lower deck was only used on these two Daimlers, a feature which would soon disappear.
Photo/ Roy Marshall

black, large white block capital lettering explained their significance.

The idea was that all services entering the city from further afield would be able to set down but not pick up after this point and on the outward journey they would only be able pick up and not be able to set down before the black bus stop. The arrangement was linked to a protective fare system later and this system was rigorously enforced by the Leicester City Council until the 1970s. This was a major factor in the profitability of the Leicester Corporation transport system. Local agreements with the Midland Red were in place but all other operators were expected to abide by the rules.

There was however a weakness in the system; the Groby Road (A50). This was a sparsely populated area in the 1920s, with only the Groby Road Hospital and Gilroes Cemetery in need of any form of service. It was considered uneconomical to invest in a tram system as far out as the city boundary, so it was cut short and terminated at a point quarter of a mile past the Fosse Road junction near Woodgate, which was the site of the "Area stop sign". The last tram to Groby Road ran on 23rd January 1949.

This meant that buses entering the city from the west were able to pick up or set down as required for almost two miles within the city boundary. A very large council housing estate called New Parks was built during the 1930s adjacent to the main road and although corporation motor buses ran through the centre of the estate those living nearer the Groby Road relied mainly upon the services provided by the Midland Red and numerous private operators on the road including Browns

Blue. It was only when buses reached Fosse Road junction that the "Area stop sign" was encountered. As can be imagined there was considerable competition on this lucrative section of route, made even more interesting on Saturday afternoons and Sundays from 10.30am, when Leicester Corporation ran their Service 56 from St. Margaret's Bus Station to Gilroes Cemetery. This service had commenced operation on 1st January 1939 as L.C.T route 29 starting from Church Gate in Leicester, but from July 1941 the terminal point was altered to St. Margaret's Bus Station, stand 12. For a short time the route was renumbered to 39 before again being renumbered 56 in March 1949.

1949 was a busy year in fleet terms. An unusual purchase was a Foden PVSC6 FJU 533, with Burlingham 33 seat bodywork. This was the first fully fronted coach in the fleet, setting the standard for many similar looking vehicles, albeit in rebuilt form. At about this time a Leyland Tiger BNR 59 was rebodied by Burlingham.

Another ex-hipwell Dennis Lancet JU 698 was withdrawn in September, but this was overshadowed by the purchase of no less than five double deckers, four Leylands and one new Daimler, a 100% increase in the double deck fleet. The Leyland TD3s JF 5873, JF 5875, JF 5878 and JF 5883, with Metro Cammell 50 seat bodywork, dating from 1934, were purchased locally from Murphy Brothers (dealer) but originally operated for Leicester City Transport. The Leicester Leyland TD3s were oil engined. They compared favourably with the former

The only Foden to be operated was delivered in June 1949, registered FJU 533 it was a PVSC6 model with Burlingham FC33F bodywork. It was fitted with the "Sprag Clutch" anti-roll back system which unfortunatly gave considerable problems when new, but once sorted it was a very reliable vehicle. Photo/ Peter Yeomans

Originally placed into service by Comfy Coaches of Ibstock during April 1939, Leyland Tiger TS8 BNR 59 with Plaxton 37 seat bodywork was soon requisitioned by the W.D. It was purchased in 1940 by Brown's Blue and was later rebodied during 1949 by Burlingham of Blackpool and it is seen here setting down passengers in Sanvey Gate, Leicester during the early 1950s. **Photo/ Roy Marshall**

Warrington TD1s but the body style was certainly more modern in appearance than the "piano fronted" bodywork of the TD1s. The frontal appearance of the Metro Cammell bodies was not dissimilar to that of new vehicles being delivered to local municipalities at that time.

The Daimler was new, a CVD6 model similar to the two Brush bodied vehicles delivered previously, but this time bodied by Roberts of Horbury Junction. It was part of a cancelled order originally placed by Colchester Corporation for ten similar vehicles, five were delivered to Colchester, and four vehicles of the cancelled order were taken up by Accrington Corporation. The remaining vehicle was purchased by Brown's Blue. It carried modern looking, four bay construction bodywork. Although of excellent quality these bodies were heavy in comparison to other body builders products, making this particular vehicle less economical to run. However FNR 273 served the company well, in fact until the very end, and beyond, with another operator.

The year ended on a sad note, the first two of the Warrington Leyland TD1s ED 6463 and ED 6464 were withdrawn and scrapped on 31st December 1949. At this time fleet strength stood at about 41 vehicles; this figure included several vehicles in stock, but out of use.

Purchases in 1950 commenced during March with two identical Dennis Lancet IIIs FUT 452 and FUT 527, with Duple 35 seat bodywork, followed by another unusual purchase in April, a Leyland Comet GAY 459, with Burlingham 33 seat bodywork. This was a normal control coach in many

Formally Leicester 272, this 1934 Leyland TD3 JF 5875 with Metro-Camell bodywork was one of five similar vehicles purchased during 1949/50. The three Warrington TD1's and the five Leicester TD3s were the only double deckers not to receive platform doors.
Photo/ Unkown

ways similar to a Bedford OB, but larger and heavier in construction. Finally in June a fifth former Leicester Leyland TD3 JF 5008, with Metro Cammell R bodywork was purchased from Murphy Brothers (dealer); this time part of an earlier batch dating from 1933.

Withdrawal of the two ex-Warner Bedfords CNR 362 and CNR 480, took place in February and March respectively and also the last former Warrington Leyland TD1 ED 6560, was withdrawn and scrapped. The second of the Bedford OWBs, CNR 436, supplied new in 1944 was taken out of service in July, followed by a similar vehicle this time formally owned by Hipwell of Ibstock.

After the end of fuel rationing on 26th May 1950, a fully revised service timetable was introduced in September 1950. This reflected the increase in passengers since the end of the Second World War. Excursions, tours and private hire contracts were all on the increase. Day trips to the coast were very popular with the Lincolnshire resorts of Cleethorpes, Mablethorpe and Skegness, the last being the most popular. There were no motorways in those days, a trip to the Lincolnshire coast took about three and a half hours including a stop, with Great Yarmouth or Blackpool taking about five and a half hours.

We will see in the next chapter how coach travel would change and how Lawrence Brown would deal with the new challenges facing the bus and coach industry.

Photographed when new before delivery Daimler CVD6 FNR 273 stands outside the Roberts bodyworks in Horbury Junction, Wakefield, Yorkshire. It was fitted with platform doors during 1952 in Brown's workshops.
Photo/ Omnibus Society Collection

Seen working on hire to Trent in Nottingham, Dennis Lancet III FUT 527 with Duple oachwork was supplied new in March 1950. It is noticeable that the side flash is finished in ivory, not all coaches were treated in this manner, a red side flash was also used. Regular driver Eric Partner reverses into place under the direction of the duty inspector. **Photo/ Richard Butler**

Brown's Blue were well known for purchasing "one off" vehicles, this Leyland Comet CPO1 GAY 459 with Burlingham bodywork was delivered in April 1950. **Photo/ Richard Butler**

Former Hipwell Dennis Lancet AAY 6 is seen here in service after repainting into Brown's Blue livery, the location is thought to be the junction of Main Street and Station Road, Bagworth. **Photo/ Omnibus Society Collection**

CHAPTER V

INCLUDING THE DRIVER

January 1951 To June 1954

In common with many other manufacturers, Leyland Motors had been designing and developing an underfloor engine chassis for single deck use, until the Second World War halted all further development.

In 1950 the Leyland Royal Tiger was introduced. It was an immediate success, the forward entrance and driver/passenger contact made possible placing the engine under the floor were both obvious advantages for either coaching and stage carriage use. Manufacturers such as AEC and Sentinel had developed their own designs but Leyland had the most success with sales at this time.

Many operators were keen to take advantage of these new designs as the traditional half cab coaches were awkward to operate when passenger contact was needed, these new designs brought the driver inside the vehicle making liaison with party organisers much easier.

Photographed before delivery outside Duple Coachworks in 1951, Leyland Royal Tiger PSU1/11 GUT 398 is fitted with a Duple Roadmaster body. Designed to resemble the American Greyhound coaches of the period, narrow windows and the use of polished aluminium brightwork set this vehicle apart from other coaches in the Brown's Blue fleet.
Photo/ Omnibus Society Collection

GUT 398 soon became the "flagship" of the fleet; even so, it was still used, when required, on service work. It is seen here in St. Margaret's Bus Station, Leicester. Photo/ R. H. G. Simpson

In June 1951 the company took delivery of its first "underfloor engined" coach, a Leyland Royal Tiger PSU1/11 GUT 398 with Duple Roadmaster 41 seat bodywork. This was by far a very different vehicle to anything operated before. The strong American influence in the design was unmistakable and the use of polished aluminium strips on the body sides and the shallow side windows were reminiscent of the Greyhound coach in America. This vehicle became the "flagship" of the fleet throughout the fifties, pictures of it appeared on timetables, letterheads and other company literature.

In August and September of that year two similar vehicles, but this time of AEC manufacture were delivered, these were based on the Regal Mk IV chassis carrying more conservative Yeates bodywork GUT 399 and GUT 400 respectively. Centre entrance bodywork was another departure from the norm in the Brown's Blue fleet. These three vehicles would ultimately be used on stage carriage services in their later lives and the central entrance would certainly be more difficult to operate on these duties.

A return to what was a more conventional vehicle at that time, was in the form of a second hand Dennis Lancet II JL 3733, with Willowbrook bodywork purchased in October from the Ministry of Supply, this vehicle was re-registered HAY 601 before entering service.

Finally in December another forward entrance coach was purchased. This time a Bedford SB chassis was chosen with Duple Vega bodywork HJU 434. The main difference with the Bedford chassis to the Leyland and AEC products was the position of the engine. Bedford kept the engine upright at the front of the chassis which

Shortly after the Leyland was delivered, two new AEC Regal IV chassis were purchased and bodied at Yeates. GUT 399 and GUT 400 were delivered in September and August 1951 respectively. **Photo/ Roy Marshall**

Taken outside the Ibstock garage, Bedford OWB DRY 777 with Duple Vista bodywork was purchased with the business of J. H. Hill on the 1st of January 1952. Originally it carried a bus body but was given a new coach body by Duple in 1948. **Photo/ Mike Sutcliffe MBE**

Formally Hill's Bedford SB HBC 634, with Duple Vega C31F bodywork stands alongside BMMO S6 3042 in St. Margaret's Bus Station, Leicester. **Photo/ R. F. Mack**

meant that the engine cover protruded into the passenger area. Engine noise needed to be suppressed by plenty of insulation on the engine cover.

To make way for these new arrivals three pre-war Bedford WTBs AJU 230, BAY 18 and AUT 287 were taken out of service, as well as one of the ex-Warner Leyland Tiger TS1s WW 6814 and the TS2 FV 1550, also the first of the ex-Leicester Leyland TD3s JF 5883, was withdrawn prematurely after turning on its side in a serious accident at Ibstock in July. Fortunately there were no serious injuries, but the bus was very badly damaged. Ironically this was the second of this batch of vehicles to end its days in similar circumstances as number 286 turned on its side in 1946 whilst still in LCT service.

The Brush bodied Daimlers appeared with painted side adverts at this time and the ex-Leicester TD3s received adverts on the rear panels, features that would become more commonplace a few years later on the rest of the double deck fleet.

The small business of J.H. Hill of 45, Duncan Road, Leicester was acquired on 1st of January 1952. This was a little unusual as previous purchases had been kept roughly within the company's operating area, but Hill's held licences to operate excursions and tours from the Coach Stand in Humberstone Gate, Leicester, this was a very lucrative operating base.

Numerous operators ran holiday services, day excursions, afternoon and evening Tours. Advanced bookings could be made at an independent booking office which was adjacent to the stand. At weekends operators running excursions and tours would park their coaches in "herringbone

This very rare photograph has been carefully restored by Paul Banbury, it shows Daimler CVD6 FNR 273 in its original livery standing in Hinckley Town centre, it is about to depart to Coalville on the busy service taken over from Hipwells.
Photo/ Keith Wortley Collection

Leicester fleet number 280 a 1934 Leyland TD3 with Metro-Cammell H26/24R bodywork is seen here at Abbey Park Road Depot during wartime. It is fitted with Anti-Blast netting on the windows, White painted wing edges and the regulation blanking out of the city name. This vehicle was one of four to be purchased by Brown's Blue during September 1949. Sadly this vehicle had a short life with Brown's, it was withdrawn in July 1951 following a serious accident.
Photo/ Leicester City Transport A.P. Newland Collection.

This nearside view of Brush bodied Daimler CVD6 EJU 541, shows clearly the rear platform doors fitted during 1952, the destination boxes over the platform and on the rear panel had not been removed at this time. Photo/ Roy Marshall

fashion" and place blackboards at the front of their vehicles detailing in chalk where they were going, the time and most importantly the price.

At this time Hill's operated four vehicles, but only one entered the Brown fleet, a 1944 Bedford OWB DRY 777, which had been re-bodied in 1948 with a Duple Vista body. There were also two Bedford OB's ERY 360 and FRY 684 the second of which was sold shortly afterwards, and a Bedford SB HBC 634 which remained in service with a new company L.D. Brown t/a J. H. Hill of Ashby Road, Markfield eventually being integrated into the Brown fleet by the 1st of July 1954. However Brown's Blue vehicles appeared from time to time on hire to Hills whenever required. Hills premises in Grace Road were also purchased and subsequently used as an outstation by Brown's Blue after July 1st 1954.

The last remaining Bedford WTB AAY 676 in the Brown fleet at that time was withdrawn in April but the main focus of attention was that of the double deck fleet. Ever since the introduction of double deckers in 1946 the "open rear" platform was the subject of some concern, the comfort of passengers sitting in the immediate area of the rear platform in the lower saloon was not acceptable. Also the conductor's safety was at risk when working in the area, especially during the winter months on exposed sections of the routes.

In 1952 the three Daimlers were chosen in turn and taken into the company workshops to receive rear platform doors. These were of the "hand operated" type to be controlled by the conductor. These were an immediate success, regular passengers would soon learn to open and close the doors behind them when the conductor was busy collecting fares elsewhere on the

Roberts bodied Daimler CVD6 FNR 273 also received platform doors at the same time; it is seen here in Markfield garage yard. **Photo/ R. F. Mack**

vehicle. However the ex-Leicester TD3s were not destined to receive doors, perhaps their relatively shorter future with the company was the reason, although one did remain in service until mid-1955 and no doubt the passengers and conductor thought they had drawn the short straw when travelling on this vehicle. Most future second hand double deck purchases would receive rear platform doors at either the Markfield or Ibstock workshops before entering service, although there were exceptions.

1953 would be a very important year for the nation and Brown's Blue as the Coronation would occupy the thoughts of the public at large, but Lawrence Brown was turning his thoughts to expanding his business and to vehicle replacement.

Awaiting a departure to Whitwick, JF 5875 a former Leicester Leyland TD3 with Metro-Cammell bodywork stands alongside BMMO S8 3228 which is loading for Heather via Ibstock. **Photo/ Unknown**

Rear views are not common, neither are photos taken on Christmas Day but add to this the fact that both vehicles were to see further service together in the Brown's Blue fleet makes this photo unique. London Transport Daimler CWA6 GLX 905 (D19) and HGC 292 (D165) stand alongside each other at Morden Station on December 25th 1952.
Photo/ Alan B Cross

In April 1953 four London Transport Daimler CWA6 double deckers HGC 288, HGC 292, HGC 296 and HGF 806, dating from 1946 were purchased with Duple bodywork to a slightly relaxed design featuring a rounded rear roof dome and split rear upper emergency window. Hand operated platform doors were fitted before entering service and the side destination boxes panelled over.

Freshly painted and about to enter service at Ibstock Daimler HGC 292 (D165) was the last of this type to remain in service. All Daimlers received chrome radiator surrounds before entering service bringing them into line with earlier Daimlers in the fleet.
Photo/ R Hannay

Also entering service at the same time were the two ex-Hills Bedfords mentioned earlier, plus a new Bedford SB JNR 926, with Yeates Riviera bodywork.

Another company purchased at this time was that of William Parsons, of Main Street, Stanton–under-Bardon. Licences and services were acquired and three vehicles were taken into the Brown fleet, two

Former LT Daimler HGC 288 (D161), stands next to BMMO D5B 3872 with Brush bodywork awaiting journeys to Whitwick and Heather respectively during 1954. **Photo/ Roy Marshall**

Taken standing outside the Ibstock garage, Daimler HGF 806 (D179) was later heavily rebuilt with sliding windows replacing the half-drop units. **Photo/ Roy Marshall**

Purchased by Brown's Blue in July 1953, Bedford SB with Yeates Riviera bodywork stands on the Humberstone Gate Coach Stand in Leicester, on the 24th January 1959. **Photo/ Richard Butler**

Delivered to Parson of Stanton-u-Bardon in March 1950, Dennis Lancet III FUT 777 with Yeates bodywork entered the Brown fleet in August 1953. It is seen on 31st January 1959 working a "Football Special" in Western Boulevard, Leicester. **Photo/ Richard Butler**

Bedford OB's DUT 149 and KNN 148 one with Duple Vista bodywork and the other bearing Plaxton FC30F bodywork and also a Dennis Lancet III FUT 777, with Yeates bodywork.

The first of a number of rebuilds commenced at about this time. The pre-war AEC Regal HRF 102 purchased in 1940 was totally stripped, the chassis was refurbished and lengthened to 30ft and a new AEC engine was fitted. The chassis was then dispatched to Yeates at Loughborough for a new full-front 39 seat body.

HRF 102, a 1939 AEC Regal was purchased in 1940 and ran with its original Harrington body until 1953, at this time the body was removed and scrapped, the chassis was extended and fitted with an AEC 7.7 oil engine, then sent to Yeates at Loughborough and fitted with a body. It is seen on 24th October 1960 in Markfield (Main Street). Photo/ Richard Butler

During September and October of 1953 negotiations between the Midland Red and Brown's Blue were taking place, involving the Coalville to Hinckley service, although each route varied from the other on the middle section of their respective routes, the terminal points were nearly the same. Both companies were proposing to put on extra services; the focus of attention was mainly the 09.40 a.m. ex- Bagworth journey proposed by Midland Red, Brown's requested that this should be put back 10 minutes to 09.50 a.m.

In December of that year two further London Transport Daimler CWA6s GLX 905 and GYE 64, entered service, both had Duple bodywork, but this time dating from 1944 and 1945 respectively, these were from earlier batches of Daimlers delivered to London Transport and featured the "lobster back" utility rear roof domes and in the case of GYE 64 a single rear upper deck emergency window common to early utility bodies. Also at the same time a similar vehicle from Southport Corporation EWM 372 entered the fleet, although there is a slight difference of opinion as to when exactly. All Daimlers were fitted with a chrome radiator surround which did enhance their frontal appearance and also platform doors were fitted, bringing them into line with the existing Daimlers in the fleet.

These purchases sealed the fate of three more of the ex-Leicester Leyland TD3s JF

One of two "Lobster Back" Daimler GLX 905 (D19) was purchased from London Transport by Brown's in December 1953, it is seen here about to leave Marlborough Square, Coalville on the frequent service to Ibstock. Photo/ Roy Marshall

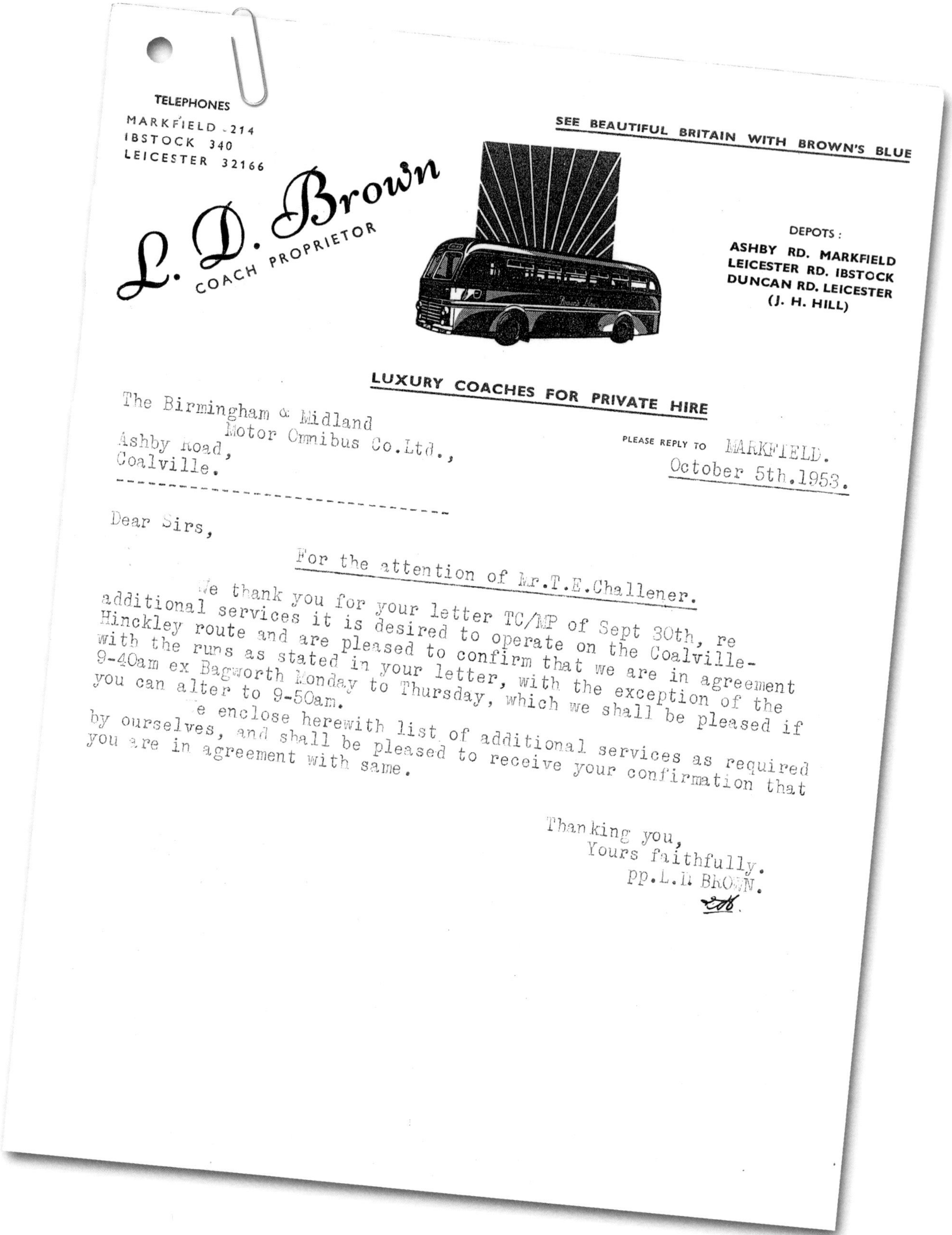

TELEPHONES
MARKFIELD 214
IBSTOCK 340
LEICESTER 32166

SEE BEAUTIFUL BRITAIN WITH BROWN'S BLUE

L. D. Brown
COACH PROPRIETOR

DEPOTS:
ASHBY RD. MARKFIELD
LEICESTER RD. IBSTOCK
DUNCAN RD. LEICESTER
(J. H. HILL)

LUXURY COACHES FOR PRIVATE HIRE

The Birmingham & Midland
Motor Omnibus Co.Ltd.,
Ashby Road,
Coalville.

PLEASE REPLY TO MARKFIELD.
October 5th.1953.

Dear Sirs,

For the attention of Mr.T.E.Challener.

We thank you for your letter TC/MP of Sept 30th, re additional services it is desired to operate on the Coalville-Hinckley route and are pleased to confirm that we are in agreement with the runs as stated in your letter, with the exception of the 9-40am ex Bagworth Monday to Thursday, which we shall be pleased if you can alter to 9-50am.

We enclose herewith list of additional services as required by ourselves, and shall be pleased to receive your confirmation that you are in agreement with same.

Thanking you,
Yours faithfully.
PP.L.D BROWN.

Omnibus Society Collection

Also seen in Marlborough Square, Coalville at the same location (see lower right photo page 55), the other "lobster back" Daimler CWA6 GYE 64 (D74), the earlier design can clearly be seen in this photograph. **Photo/ Richard Butler**

Odd man out amongst the Daimlers was this former Southport EWM 372; virtually identical to its London Transport counterparts this vehicle was easily identified by its front destination layout. **Photo/ Roy Marshall**

This aerial view of St. Margaret's Bus Station was taken in the early fifties possibly on a Bank Holiday Monday; the queue in the foreground is waiting for the Midland Red service to Newtown Linford (Bradgate Park). Two of the ex-Leicester Leyland TD3s purchased by Brown's Blue can be seen entering the loading bays. **Photo/ Leicester Mercury**

The last two vehicles to be delivered to the "old company" were two Bedford SBG coaches KAY 674 and KAY 675 both fitted with Yeates Riviera C38F bodywork. The latter is seen here at Ibstock garage.
Photo/ Mike Sutcliffe MBE

5873, JF 5875 and JF 5878, which were scrapped shortly afterwards. One of the former Hipwell Dennis's RC 1525 was also withdrawn at this time and is presumed to have been scrapped.

1954 would prove to be a significant year for the company, further expansion and a change in company title was about to take place, but the final new deliveries would enter service with the "old" company, these were two Bedford SBGs KAY 674 and KAY 675, with Yeates Riviera bodywork. They both entered service in January, one of each being allocated to Markfield and Ibstock depots respectively.

CHAPTER VI

LIMITED COMPANY

July 1954 to July 1957

On 1st July 1954 the status of the business changed, the company was now a limited company which was formed by acquiring the companies of L.D.Brown, L.D.Brown - t/a J.H.Hill, and a new acquisition Joseph Albert Rudin - t/a C.Rudin & Sons.The new company title was now **BROWNS BLUE COACHES LTD**.

Public notices appeared in the local press announcing details of the new company; one such notice referring to the Markfield (Shaw Lane) depot is set out below:-

> ***BROWNS BLUE COACHES LTD***
> *(532395), Registered April 23 1954*
> *Shaw lane, Markfield, near Leicester.*
> *Nominal capital £25,000 in £1 shares.*
> *Directors to be appointed by the*
> *subcribers L.D. Brown, Silver Lay,*
> *Markfield Road, Groby, Leicestershire.*
> *R.L. Brown, 100, Leicester Road,*
> *Ibstock, Leicestershire.*

There was no mention of Laurie Browns two other sons at this point, but all three became shareholders along with the remaining immediate family. Norman and Reginald both worked within the company at Markfield and Ibstock respectively and the third son Terence was still serving as an apprentice at a Loughborough firm of coachbuilders. At this time the Shaw Lane, Markfield depot was managed by Mr J. W. Neale and the Ibstock depot by Mr T. Underwood.

As I mentioned on my introduction page a small but significant detail to arise from this event was the omission of the apostrophe before the "s" in Browns; this was gradually altered on all vehicles and Company stationary. However local newspapers still printed the name in the old way until the company ceased trading in 1963. Hence,

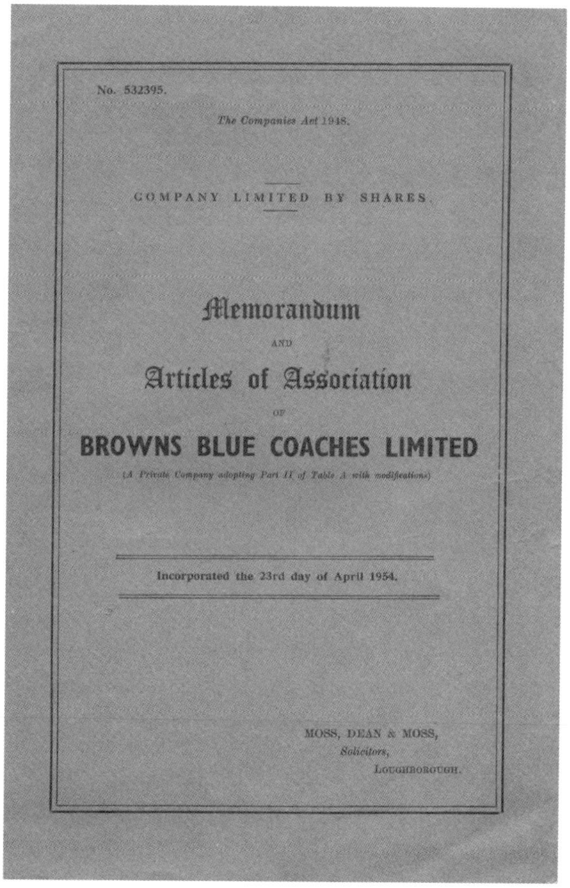
No. 532395.
The Companies Act 1948.
COMPANY LIMITED BY SHARES.
Memorandum
AND
Articles of Association
OF
BROWNS BLUE COACHES LIMITED
(A Private Company adopting Part II of Table A with modifications)
Incorporated the 23rd day of April 1954.
MOSS, DEAN & MOSS,
Solicitors,
LOUGHBOROUGH.

Articles of Association, documents.
Supplied/ Wynn & Norman Brown

Dating from 1934 this ex-Rudin Dennis Lancet, VJ 6068 was rebodied by Yeates during 1948 and fitted with an AEC 7.7 oil engine, the original seats were retained and reupholstered. **Photo/ Unkown**

from this point on in this book, I shall use the later version of grammar unless when quoting events before April 23rd 1954 or newspaper articles.

The acquisition of G. Rudin and Sons brought five vehicles into the Browns fleet, but the premises in the northern section of Melbourne Road, Ibstock were not purchased. The vehicles involved were a pre-war Dennis Lancet VJ 6068, which had been rebodied by Yeates and fitted with an AEC 7.7 oil engine, two Bedford WTBs AJU 879 and BNR 631, with Duple bodywork, one Bedford OWB AMS 257 with SMT bodywork, which was withdrawn immediately and a Bedford OB ENR 294 with Duple Vista bodywork.

The austere measures in place since the Second World War were now slowly being relaxed, many everyday commodities which had been rationed were now becoming freely available, items such as televisions, radios and even washing machines were all considered as luxuries at the time. More and more family cars were being purchased as all of these items were becoming widely available. American influences were beginning to make themselves felt within society Rock and Roll music, Elvis, Coffee Bars, Teddy Boys and pastel shades, also everything seemed to be chromed!. A fresh, bright outlook on life was taking over, optimism was the key, the war years and the austere post-war period had certainly taken its toll, but times were changing. In general people were able to afford to go out more, this all had a positive effect upon travel, in particular the bus industry, passenger usage had increased to unprecedented numbers and business was good.

Taken outside the Ibstock Depot, former Rudin Bedford WTB, AJU 879 with Duple bodywork never received Browns livery, it was sold shortly afterwards to Desford Colliery Sports Club in August 1954. **Photo/ R. F. Mack**

Former Rudin Bedford OB ENR 294 with Duple bodywork is seen here in St. Margaret's Bus Station, Leicester. **Photo/ Mike Sutcliffe MBE**

To take advantage of the increase in prosperity, businesses began to invest in many forms of advertising. Browns Blue were quick to take advantage of this extra income and so many more advertisements began to appear on the double deck fleet. Local businesses had adverts painted onto each side of the vehicles and demand was such that smaller adverts were placed either side of the front destination display, on the rear panels and on the rear quarters. The ex-Toone Dennis Lancet ANR 216, purchased in 1939 was the only withdrawal this year, it passed to Daisy of Broughton.

1955 was a busy year for the garage staff at Markfield and Ibstock, there were three mechanics and one bodybuilder at each garage. The Dennis coaches came under scrutiny, four vehicles in all were involved, a former Hipwell Dennis and a similar ex-Warner vehicle both passed to Daisy of Broughton. The other two were taken out of service, AAY 6 and JU 7854 had their bodies removed and the chassis were extended and refurbished. They were fitted with AEC 7.7 oil engines and then taken over to Yeates at Loughborough for re-bodying with new full-front bodywork. As testament to the thorough mechanical work carried out on the reconditioned chassis the ministry inspectors awarded these vehicles with a very long certificate of fitness, although in fairness the bodies were built as new units. Nonetheless this is an example of the quality of workmanship carried out at the Browns Blue workshops.

Dennis Lancet II DRF 530 was one of three similar vehicles sold to Daisy, Broughton during 1954/55 the other two were ANR 216 and JU 3054. **Photo/ Roy Marshall**

After its rebuilding, what was originally a Hipwell vehicle, Dennis Lancet II AAY 6, poses for the camera, on vacant land near St. Margaret's Bus Station. **Photo/ R. G. Simpson**

The only other withdrawal came in July when the last ex-Leicester TD3 JF 5008, was de-licenced and sold to a showman. This would become quite significant; the double deck fleet now consisted totally of buses fitted with pre-select gearboxes, considered by the Ministry of Transport as "semi-automatic". Ministry regulations demanded that to drive any type of PSV vehicle a full double deck "stick" licence test needed to be taken.

Two Lancets were rebodied at the same time; JU 7854 began its life in the Warner fleet, passing to Brown's in January 1948. AEC oil engines were fitted to both vehicles at the time of the rebuild. **Photo/ Roy Marshall**

A serious shortage of platform staff within the industry had been a problem for several years. Locally companies such as Midland Red were advertising on a weekly basis in the local press, but their wage structure was no competition to the local manufacturing industries and the numerous coal mines in the area. The higher wages were more attractive to a local workforce who were keen to use these extra funds to finance the purchase of the luxuries we have just been talking about.

Unless a licence was already held, new employees were usually employed as conductors and after a short period of

The only Commer in the fleet, NJU 948 with Duple bodywork stands in Western Boulevard, Leicester working a "Football Special". It is wearing the later coach livery, the design of the Duple bodywork made it necessary to place the fleet name much lower than normal. Photo/ Derek Westall

familiarisation with the job, suitable employees would be given the opportunity to retrain as drivers. From the companies point of view it was most desirable that drivers were trained on a double deck vehicle with a manual "stick" gearbox, enabling the company to take full advantage of the drivers capabilities when utilising their labour for the variety of duties worked by the company. A new driver passing his test on a pre-select vehicle would only be qualified to drive such a vehicle, therefore he would not be able to drive any of the single deck vehicles in the fleet, which were all of the standard manual gearbox type. We will see later, at least one double decker with manual gearbox would be retained whenever possible for this purpose.

All vehicle purchases during 1956 were very unusual. In May a new Commer Avenger III NJU 948 with Duple Vega C41F bodywork entered service. This was fitted with the unmistakable two stroke engine and was only the second vehicle of this manufacture to be operated it was followed by an ex-Maidstone and District Leyland TD7 GKL 765, with Weymann bodywork dating from 1940. This vehicle was fitted with platform doors before entering service. Although purchased with an engine defect it lasted until October 1957, when an AEC 7.7 complete with gearbox was fitted, taken from one of the ex-Hipwell Dennis Lancets, this then being scrapped. As I mentioned before, the conventional manual gearbox would become very useful.

Former Maidstone and District Leyland TD7 GKL 765 with Weymann bodywork stands in Marlborough Square, Coalville. Purchased with a faulty engine, GKL soldiered on for a short time until the AEC engine and gearbox from Dennis Lancet JU 7525 were fitted in November 1957. **Photo/ Roy Marshall**

In November the former Daimler CD650 Demonstrator KHP 998, was purchased, formally operated by Beckett of Bucknall

Taken at the Commercial Motor Show, Earls Court in 1951, Daimler CD650 Demonstrater later passed to Beckett of Bucknall, Staffs, before being purchased by Browns Blue in December 1956. **Photo/ Commercial Motor**

and originally used by Daimler for demonstration purposes. This vehicle was powered by a 10.6 litre diesel engine, which proved to be, not the most fuel efficient vehicle in the fleet. However no one could deny that it was a powerful beast, an image further enhanced by the Roe bodywork built to export specifications. This was the first and only 8ft wide double decker in the fleet, featuring extended louvres over the windows for extra shading in sunnier, brighter climates, a fitment of little use in the rugged terrain of west Leicestershire.

The end of food rationing in 1954 had signalled the return to some sort of normality, however international affairs were still in turmoil and the Cold War was at its height. A significant event took place

The former Daimler CD650 Demonstrator KHP 998 is seen here outside Ibstock garage. It was used with an open rear platform as seen here until June 1958 when manual operated doors were fitted at Markfield garage. **Photo/ Peter Yeomans**

on July 26th 1956 when both Britain and the U.S. announced that they were withdrawing all funding of the Aswan High Dam in Egypt. President Nasser of Egypt responded immediately by nationalising the Suez Canal, a blockade was put in place which had a devastating effect upon fuel supplies to the west, the majority of oil tankers delivering oil to Europe and the U.S.A. from the Middle Eastern oil fields passed through the canal. They now needed to divert around Cape Horn a much longer and more hazardous route. Fuel rationing was re-introduced in Britain in the autumn of 1956 and in common with most other operators Browns Blue needed to conserve fuel. An emergency timetable was introduced on December 17th 1956 which operated through until May 1957.

The British Government led by Anthony Eden along with support from France and Israel embarked upon military intervention which although successful in the military sense, was a complete disaster politically. This incensed world opinion including that of the United States, resulting in the resignation of Anthony Eden in January 1957.

The Midland Red had recently "flexed its muscles" by purchasing a number of important independent operators in the Leicestershire area. In response several medium sized private operators decided to form an organisation called The Midlands Area Coach and Transport Association, which was based in Rutland Street, Leicester.

Lawrence Brown, T.H. Mills of Gibsons, Sydney Astill, George Hylton and many other operators became founder members of the association. Many other operators working within the county and neighbouring counties also joined. This was needed to facilitate cross boundary contracts and services. The aim of the organisation was to consolidate works, school and private hire contracts as well as stage carriage services under one protective umbrella. Contracts would be then allotted to members according to their operating area as far as was possible. Coverage of work which for whatever reason could not be honoured at any particular time was passed onto other operators within the group on a temporary basis, until normal coverage could be resumed.

Stage Carriage licences were held by the individual operator, but any applications to the local Traffic Area for changes to routes, fares, or timetables etc, could be handled by the association if required. At any Traffic Court appearances operators could also be represented by the association. This gave members a stronger unified position when negotiating working arrangements alongside those of the larger operators. A full individual company stationery service was also available to members.

Another service provided was the supply and maintenance of ticket machines and tickets printed with individual company details could also be supplied. In later years the organisation became involved with ordering and delivering spare parts for its members and an arrangement was agreed with Birds of Stratford for the supply of parts which was especially useful for those operators who had purchased former London Transport vehicles. Birds had built up large stocks of ex-LT spares and vehicles which were in turn sold onto provincial operators throughout the country and beyond. This organisation was much respected by the larger local bus companies, and the temptation to "ride roughshod" over smaller operators was very much reduced. In later years the association would become known as the P.S.V. Ltd.

Browns Blue had operated numerous works and school contracts for many years. The original service operated by Laurie Brown, from Markfield and Stanton to Anstey (Shoe Factories) was still operating, as well as the Grieve Needle Company contract which involved two buses from Leicester each day. The large English Electric factory which was situated a few miles to the south of Leicester at Whetstone, was served by three buses each day. These had been parked overnight at St. Margaret's Bus Station for some time, but it was difficult to lock these vehicles up and on more than one occasion unwanted visitors had used the coaches for overnight accommodation. Therefore a secure yard in Freeschool Lane, Leicester was later used as well as a similar property in New Park Street, Leicester.

Several colliery services to Bagworth, Ellistown and Desford ran twice daily and Ibstock garage supplied five buses for various services to Clutsam and Kemp's elastic factory in Coalville,. Two vehicles were used on contracts to factories in Earl Shilton and one to the Desford Tubes factory. These services also served Desford, Bagworth and Nailstone collieries.

Stage Carriage services operated by Markfield Garage from Leicester were in direct competition with several other operators as far as Glenfield Turn and Markfield. From there on services split and became much simpler, the Ibstock, Heather and Measham services turned left and on to Stanton-under-Bardon and beyond running parallel with the Victory service.

Midland Red dominated services from the Markfield (Flying Horse) roundabout westwards towards Bardon and Coalville. Browns Whitwick service turned right at this point north westwards towards Copt Oak and Greenhill before descending into Whitwick. Responsibility for the Hinckley, Ibstock, Ellistown, Ashby and Coalville area Stage Carriage services fell to the Ibstock Garage, although it was not unknown for routes to swap over from time to time. This relieved some boredom and familiarised staff with the route network as a whole. Former driver John Shillcot recalls that fourteen trips a day on the Ibstock to Coalville service driving a "crash gearbox" decker was not to be taken lightly.

A full season of tours and excursions were operated from both garages, as well as from Humberstone Gate, Leicester, using the licenses acquired with the Hill business. The need for "ON HIRE TO J.H.HILL" stickers was no longer required. Browns Blue Coaches lined up on the coach stand in their own right along with other operators. Jack Parry was in charge of Browns Blue's operations at Humberstone Gate. He made sure that coaches left on time and persuaded intending passengers of the benefits of travelling with Browns Blue. Although based at Markfield, driver Harry Knight actually worked from Hill's old depot in Duncan Road, Leicester, covering much of the private hire and excursion work. There were several other drivers who lived in Leicester and they were allowed to take their coaches home in order to make an early start the next day.

Angling clubs always dealt with driver Dick Clapham for their early morning fishing trips to the Fens. These were long days for the driver especially if he had no interest in fishing. The fishermen often returned to the coach covered in mud, and after the compulsory stop at the pub on the way home the driver still had to clean the coach out for the next day's duties.

Returning to fleet matters, although the bodywork was built to a relatively high standard at the time, the two Brush bodied Daimlers were now beginning to show signs of body frame movement. Built after the war, the materials used were still considered to be of sub-standard quality due to severe shortages, some of the wood was unseasoned "green", this had a tendency to warp when drying out. The bodies would suffer water ingress which in turn caused further misalignment, opening windows would jam and in severe cases crack, body panels would also bend and buckle giving the vehicle an ungainly appearance. Small metal brackets were fitted next to the front upper deck windows; this was only a temporary measure until a more permanent repair could be carried out.

It was decided to rebuild EJU541 first, followed by FAY 517 later. All glazing was replaced with rubber mounted units, the panel work below the lower windows was modified, as a result the lower large section waist rail was replaced a feature characteristic to these bodies. Panel work between the wheels was modified to finish further down nearer to the ground, displacing the need for the lower guard rail, a legal requirement on all double deck

Seen departing St. Margaret's Bus Station, Leicester and making its way to Stanton-u-Bardon is Daimler CVD6 EJU 541 it was completely rebuilt using rubber mounted glazing. Photo/ Roy Marshall

vehicles at that time. This made these two vehicles look bulky, which to my mind spoilt their overall appearance. A larger destination display was also fitted at this time. A full repaint was carried out, the deep blue was extended to most of the vehicle with the exception of the band between decks, mudguards and wheels which were finished in red.

These were not the only problems encountered with the Daimlers. Engine overheating was a common problem with these vehicles. Leicester City Transport had placed a total of twenty nine similar Daimlers into service and had suffered constant problems of this nature. The Browns Blue Daimlers also suffered overheating problems, albeit to a lesser degree, but usually only on the outbound journey from Leicester which was a long climb throughout its length until Greenhill was reached which was only two miles from Whitwick. There were no problems in the opposite direction where revs were obviously kept down.

Transport Historian and former L.C.T apprentice diesel fitter Paul Banbury explains his theory to the cause of this problem. He remembers working on the Daimlers back in the early sixties and says that it was due to the constant "stop start" nature of the city routes and the long narrow radiator. The efficiency of the cooling system was impaired and it was not unusual to see these vehicles running with the engine side panel laid open and resting on the inner section of the front wing.

Below is a list of some of the services licensed by the Traffic Commissioners for the East Midland Traffic Area, to be operated by Browns Blue at March 1957:-

TER 4614/1 Stanton-under-Bardon (Crown Inn) to Anstey Via Shaw Lane, Markfield, and Newtown Linford. Monday to Saturday

TER 4614/2 Ibstock (Hastings Arms) to Nailstone Colliery. Weekdays Via Belchers Bar.

TER 4614/3 Markfield (The Green) to Loughborough (Packhorse Lane) Via Shaw Lane, Copt Oak, Charley Cross Roads, and Nanpantan. Thursdays

TER 4614/8 Newtown Linford to Ellistown and Desford Collieries Via Field Head, Markfield and Stanton. Weekdays

TER 4614/9 Donnington-Le-Heath to Coalville (Marlborough Square) Via Cresent Road, and Highfields. Monday to Friday

TER 4614/10* Coalville (Marlborough Square) to Bagworth (Barrel Inn) Via Hugglescote and Ellistown. Monday to Saturday

TER 4614/11* Coalville (Marlborough Square) to Hinckley (The Borough) Via Hugglescote, Ellistown, Bagworth, Newbold Verdon, Kirby Mallory, Earl Shilton and Barwell. Daily

TER 4614/12 Ibstock (Hastings Arms) to Smisby (Coal Lane) Via High Street, Heather, Normanton, Packington, and Ashby-de-la-Zouch. (Terminates at Ashby on Sunday, Monday, Tuesday, Thursday and Friday.) Daily

TER 4614/14* Stanton-under-Bardon to Coalville (Memorial Square) Via Shaw Lane and Bardon Hill. Daily

TER 4614/15 Donnington-Le-Heath (Donnington Arms) to Earl Shilton (Hill Top) Via Nailstone, Barlestone Turn, Osbaston Turn, Cadeby, Stapleton and Barwell. Weekdays

TER 4614/20 Leicester (L.M.R. Station, London Road) to Oadby (Racecourse) Racedays

TER 4614/16* Ibstock (Hastings Arms) to Coalville (Marlborough Square) Via Colliery Lane, Ellistown, Hugglescote, and Halfway House. Weekdays

TER 4614/17* Ibstock (Leicester Road Garage) to Desford Colliery Village (Merry Lees). Via Ellistown and Bagworth. Weekdays

TER 4614/36* Leicester (St. Margaret's Bus Stn) to Stanton-under-Bardon Via Groby, Markfield and Cliffe Hill. Daily

TER 4616/37*	Leicester (St. Margaret's Bus Stn) to Whitwick (Market Place) Via Groby, Markfield, Shaw Lane and Copt Oak. Daily
TER 4616/39	Heather (Crown Hotel) to Whitwick Colliery Via Ibstock, South Hotel, Hugglescote and Coalville. Weekdays
TER 4614/42*	Leicester (St. Margaret's Bus Station) to Ibstock Via Groby, Markfield, Shaw Lane, Bardon Chapel, and Ellistown. Daily - Certain journeys onto Heather, Swepstone and Measham (Cock Spur).
TER 4614/46	Ibstock (Church) to Coalville (Grammer School). School Days

** Indicates service licensed for high bridge double deckers.*

LEICESTER CITY FOOTBALL AND SPEEDWAY SERVICES

TER 4614/4	Thringstone (The Green) to Leicester City Football Ground Home Matches Via Whitwick, Forest Rock, Copt Oak, Flying Horse, Markfield, Groby and Glenfield Turn
TER 4614/5	Whitwick to Leicester (Blackbird Road Stadium) Via Forest Rock, Copt Oak, Flying Horse, Markfield, Groby, Glenfield Turn and Fosse Road Corner. All Speedway and Stock Car meetings.
TER 4614/6	Stanton-u-Bardon to Leicester City Football Ground Via Markfield, Groby and Glenfield. Home Matches
TER 4614/13	Thornton to Leicester (Blackbird Road Stadium) Via Stanton-u-Bardon, Flying Horse, Markfield and Groby. All Speedway and Stock Car meetings.
TER 4614/41	Heather to Leicester City Football Ground Via Ibstock, Ellistown, Bardon Chapel and Flying Horse. Home Matches
TER 4614/21	Ibstock to Leicester (Blackbird Road Stadium) Via Ellistown and Hugglescote. All Speedway and Stock Car meetings.

A mixture of double deck or coaches used to meet demand.

Finally returning to fleet acquisitions, two new AEC Reliance coaches OJU 915 and ONR 771 were purchased during February and April 1957, both were fitted with Duple Britannia bodywork. They were also fitted with vacuum brakes and both vehicles served in the fleet until the takeover in 1963.

One of two similar vehicles purchased early in 1957, AEC Reliance ONR 771 with Duple Brittania bodywork stands in St. Margaret's Bus Station Station during June 1958. **Photo/ Richard Butler**

Dennis Lancet JU 6058 was withdrawn during 1957; it was sold to Hughes (Dealer) of Gomersal, near Bradford. It is seen here complete with trade plates after withdrawal. **Photo/ John Clark Collection**

Fellow operators working the A50 corridor in and out of Leicester during the middle to late fifties and early sixties.

Based at Ibstock, Windridge, Son and Riley (Victory) ran a daily service from the Measham, Heather and Ibstock area into Leicester. This Burlingham bodied AEC Regal 111 KAL 99 fleet number 14, was purchased from Robin Hood Coaches in March 1951, it passed into the Brown fleet in 1958. It is seen here about to depart to Heather from St. Margaret's Bus Station, Leicester. **Photo/ Unknown**

Hylton and Dawson ran a variety of coaches and single deck buses on their Glenfield to Leicester service. In common with the other four operators this service had operated since the nineteen twenties.

Formerly belonging to J. W. Camplin (Holme Delight) of Donington, Lincolnshire this 1946 AEC Regal ADO 513 with Harrington bodywork, was purchased by Hylton and Dawson in 1956, it awaits its next journey to Glenfield. Buses taking layover time parked towards the rear of the loading bays in St. Margaret's Bus Station, Leicester. Parked further to the rear are two Astill and Jordan vehicles in the form of a Crossley coach and an ex-East Yorkshire Leyland TD5, rebodied by Eastern Coachworks in the immediate post-war period, the distinctive "Beverly Bar" roof design can clearly be seen. **Photo/ Mike Sutcliffe MBE**

Astill and Jordan of Ratby operated various vehicles both single and double deck on their "Ratby Service". Vehicles were generally painted in a shade of mid-blue and cream, but a smart livery of turquoise blue and cream was adopted as standard in the early sixties, an example of which can be seen on this former Maidstone and District Bristol K6A HKR 42 with Weymann bodywork dating from 1947, making its way out of Leicester along Northgate Street with a healthy load. The steel "Bowstring" bridge in Northgate Street, carrying the Great Central Railway was a prominent landmark, which was not easy to miss when entering Leicester from the A50 Groby Road. The railway closed in 1969, and the bridge was eventually taken down in 1981. **Photo/ Mike Sutcliffe MBE**

It's a common misconception that Browns Blue operated services from Leicester to Coalville and the surrounding areas, however this is not strictly true. The company never actually ran a direct service from Leicester to Coalville, this was the domain of The Birmingham and Midland Motor Omnibus Company (Midland Red), locally known as "The Midland". Taken during the mid-fifties this photograph shows a BMMO FEDD type FHA 206 fleet number 2224 dating from 1938, with rebuilt Brush bodywork by Aero Engineering and Marine during 1951 featuring rubber mounted glazing. It is awaiting its next journey to Coalville via Markfield.

The adverts either side of the front destination promoting "Old Judge Tea" were a common feature of the BMMO FEDDs. In the background can be seen Brown's Blue Daimler CVD6 EJU 541, again with Brush bodywork dating from 1947. This vehicle was also extensively rebuilt in a similar manner using rubber mounted glazing by the staff at Markfield garage.
Photo/ Geoff Price Keith Wortley Collection

Colour Collection Two

IN REGULAR SERVICE

Many quality black and white photographs have been taken of Browns Blue vehicles over the years, but during the mid-fifties colour photography, although still in its infancy was becoming more commonplace. Here is a selection of photos taken by a variety of photographers depicting the heyday of Browns Blue operation.

It is inevitable that variations in colour can occur, different cameras, settings, makes of film and most of all weather conditions can affect the final print. In some ways these enthusiasts were the pioneers of modern transport photography. It is worth remembering that those were the days of carefully setting up the camera, a steady hand and plenty of patience, films ruined were costly! There was no "delete" option on those cameras.

Taken in the summer of 1960 former Sheffield AEC Megent MK111 KWB 82 with Northern Counties bodywork typifies a normal day in St. Margaret's bus station, Leicester. KWB has recently entered service with Browns Blue, you can almost smell the new paint! **Photo/ Derek Bailey Trevor Follows Collection**

The original double deck livery favoured larger areas of red, Daimler CVD6 EJU 541 with Brush bodywork is seen unloading in Gravel Street, Leicester. **Photo/ Mike Sutcliffe MBE**

Taken outside the Leicester Road depot at Ibstock in 1958 is the former Victory AEC Megal Mk IV HAY 111 with Gurney Nutting bodywork. It looks resplendant in its Browns Blue coach livery. **Photo/ Derek Bailey Trevor Follows Collection**

By stark contrast and taken in virtually the same position HAY 111 now carries the later coach livery. In my opinion the vehicle has lost much of its panache as well as both of its spotlights, a sure sign of demotion to service duties. **Photo/ Derek Bailey Trevor Follows Collection**

Showing signs of nearly ten years of regular service, the Roberts bodied Daimler is seen at Ibstock shortly before repainting. There is some doubt about the livery applied to FNR 273. All double deckers were originally painted with a red bonnet top, it appears from this photograph that the bonnet top had always been blue, but then again FNR 273 was always the odd ball in the fleet. **Photo/ Derek Bailey Trevor Follows Collection**

Always a popular location for photographers the Leicester Road depot forecourt provided easy access with unrestricted views. However this photograph was actually taken by a member of the Brown family, it shows AEC Reliance (unidentified) and three AEC RTs HLW 160, HLX 225 and HLW 151. **Photo/ Reede Brown**

Taken in Marlborough Square, Coalville is former Leicester Corporation AEC Regent DJF 323 with Weymann bodywork. Before entering service the characteristic outward sweep on the lower body panels was replaced with straight lower paneling. DJF 323 was always recognised as an Ibstock vehicle. **Photo/ Unknown**

In my opinion the later coach livery was far less attractive than the original colour scheme, former Wallace Arnold Leyland PS1/1 rebuild LNW 990 stands outside the Leicester Road, depot at Ibstock. **Photo/ Ken Jubb**

Double deckers occasionally visited Ashby de la Zouch in service, especially after the Leicester to Ibstock service was extended to Ashby via Heather, Normanton and Packington at weekends.
Former Devon General AEC Regent HTT 333 with Weymann bodywork is seen here in the Square in Ashby accompanied by a variety of Midland Red vehicles. **Photo/ Ken Jubb**

A combination of numerous quarries en route and wet days gave the garage staff major problems when trying to keep the buses clean. Taken entering Lower Churchgate Daimler CVD6 FNR 273 is seen nearing the end of its days with Browns Blue. The adverts have all but peeled off, never to be replaced and the famous BB sign in the always vacant front destination number box has now disappeared. **Photo/ Mike Sutcliffe MBE**

The final two coaches supplied in 1962 were Bedford SB5s with Harrington Crusader bodywork; they are both seen outside the Ibstock Leicester Road garage. **Photo/ Derek Bailey Trevor Follows Collection**

Making its way out of the bus station in Leicester, former Devon General AEC Regent KOD 592 starts its journey to Stanton-u-Bardon. **Photo/ Ken Jubb**

Routes terminating in Memorial Square, Coalville were those from Stanton-u-Bardon and some colliery services. AEC Regent KOD 592 is seen here outside the open air market in the winter of 1962/63. **Photo/ Ken Jubb**

Purchased with the business of J. H. Hill of Duncan Road, Leicester in June 1953 this Bedford SB HBC 634 with Duple Vega bodywork served with the fleet until the sale in March 1963. The red flash on each side was an attractive addition which helped to break up the large areas of blue. **Photo/ Derek Bailey Trevor Follows Collection**

After the last day of service on 15th March 1963 the double deck fleet was parked at Copt Oak and were soon offered for sale, after which purchasers collected their vehicles. Former LT RT HLX 225 is seen pulling out of line to start its journey to Smiths of Upper Heyford, Oxfordshire. **Photo/ Ken Jubb**

CHAPTER VII

SAD TIMES

July 1957 to 15th March 1963

If ever there was a turning point in this company's history July 1957 would surely rank as possibly the most important. For several months strike action over pay and conditions had been threatened in both the public and private sectors of the workplace nationwide. There had been an active union at Browns Blue for several years and relationships between staff and management had been good and employee loyalties towards the company were never questioned. However this left T&GWU representative Nat Spencer and his colleague at Ibstock with an unenviable predicament. The union members at both the Midland Red and Leicester City Transport were far more militant and expected the full support of local drivers employed by the smaller private operators should a strike occur.

A minimum pay rise of ten shillings (50p) per week was the demand by the union and after a heated exchange at Markfield Depot one morning in early July Lawrence Brown accepted the demand on the condition that the pay would be adjusted to the final agreed rate at the end of the dispute.

Bus services were provided with the blessing of the T&GWU, window posters stating that the bus was running with the permission of the trade union, were used on the buses to relay the message to striking pickets en route and in the terminal bus stations. The final outcome of the dispute was that the union settled for a weekly payment of a half a crown ($12^{1}/_{2}$p), a sum substantially lower than that first demanded.

Although running the business took up most of Lawrence's time, he was also a director of The Midland Area Coach and Transport Association and served on the board, but he still found time to devote several hours a week tending to local matters. Lawrence was an active member of Groby Parish Council and it was whilst representing the Council at a meeting at Market Bosworth Rural Council on 8th July 1957 he suddenly took ill and was driven home.

One of his daughters Doral was working away as a nurse in New Zealand and upon learning of her father's illness she caught the first available flight home. Unfortunately Doral did not arrive back in time; Lawrence aged 56 had passed away on Sunday 14th July without seeing her.

Lawrence was buried at St Philip and St James Church, Groby on Wednesday 17th July. The funeral was attended by many people including family, friends, work colleagues, business associates and representatives of the various local councils. Three or four coaches were present and were filled with floral tributes, Lawrence was buried alongside the main A50, the road his blue buses served so well.

Returning to the business, the two eldest sons Reginald and Norman carried on with the day to day running of the company, the

One of four Leyland PS1/1 coaches purchased from Wallace Arnold of Leeds in December 1957, KUG 3 had its original Duple body rebuilt by Wilkes and Meade to a fully fronted design retaining the original bulkhead. It is pictured here on 20th May 1958 outside the Ibstock garage. **Photo/ Richard Butler**

third son Terence was still working in Loughborough as an apprentice coachbuilder.

There were several vehicle withdrawals during 1957 including the Dennis Lancet II HAY 601, followed by two of the Tilling Stevens coaches EUT 52 and EUT 947 and finally two former Rudin vehicles, a Dennis Lancet VJ 6068 and a Bedford WTB BNR 631 which was sold to become a mobile shop. In December four ex-Wallace Arnold coaches were purchased. These were all of Leyland manufacture KUG 3 carried a Duple body, KUG 6 and KUM 621 were both bodied by Wilkes and Meade and LNW 990 was bodied by Burlingham, but rebuilt by Wilkes and Meade to a Plaxton design.

KUM 521 was virtually identical to KUG 6. All three vehicles dated from 1947. On close examination the original bulkhead can just be seen. The rather upright steering column associated with half cab vehicles can also clearly be seen. **Photo/ Unknown**

On the 26th January 1958 the associated fleet of Windridge, Sons and Riley Ltd was absorbed into the main Browns Blue operation. Six vehicles in all were involved they included, 1947 Leyland PS1/1 EAY 180 which had been re-bodied in 1950 by Yeates, two Bedford OBs FAY 675 and FUT 339 which both carried Duple Vista bodywork, an AEC Regal III KAL 99 with Burlingham bodywork, an AEC Regal IV HAY 111 with Gurney Nutting bodywork and finally a AEC Regal ADO 619 with Duple bodywork.

Although very similar in design to KUG 3, KUG 6 received a slightly modified front grill using less "bright work".
Photo/ R. H. G. Simpson

Odd one out of the four vehicles was LNW 990 dating from 1948. Wilkes and Meade rebuilt the original Burlingham body to a Plaxton fully fronted design, but without retaining the original bulkhead. As can be seen this vehicle had a much more modern outward appearance, with modified side mouldings and revised livery. It is seen here at Ibstock garage.
Photo/ John Clark Collection

1946 AEC Regal ADO 619 is seen at St. Margaret's Bus Station during the late 1950s. Originally owned by Windridge. Son and Riley of Ibstock, it entered the Brown fleet in January 1958 when the company was finally integrated into the parent company. **Photo/ Roy Marshall**

Originally delivered to Robin Hood Coaches of Nottingham during November 1948, KAL 99 an AEC Regal III with Burlingham bodywork, passed to Windridge Son and Riley in March 1951 and subsequently onto Browns Blue in January 1958. It is seen here in St. Margaret's Bus Station, Leicester. **Photo/ Roy Marshall**

Delivered new to Windridge Son and Riley in July 1951, this unusual AEC Regal IV with rare Gurney Nutting bodywork is seen outside the Ibstock garage during 1958 before repainting into Browns livery. Photo/ R. N. Hannay

All services including the football and speedway specials were integrated into the Browns Blue timetable.

Two new smaller capacity Bedfords entered service in April 1958. These were the Bedford C5Z1 model with Duple Super Vista bodywork, PUT 659 and PUT 660 normally garaged at Ibstock and Markfield respectively. Although these vehicles were delivered in the old livery they soon received the later coach livery of two tone blue.

This was the start of a large influx of vehicles made necessary by the body deterioration of the London Transport Daimlers. These buses had served the company well, several received the later livery, but sadly by this time were in need of replacement. London Transport was withdrawing its large class of AEC RT double deck vehicles, based on the AEC Regent III chassis, modified to London Transport's own specification. It has been well documented elsewhere that the success of the RT and the large scale withdrawal of the class by London Transport during the late fifties, was

Taken in Western Boulevard, Leicester, another ex-Windridge vehicle, EAY 180 a Leyland PS1/1 with Yeates bodywork, it is seen working a "Football Special".
Photo/ Mike SutcLiffe MBE

Taken on private hire duties in London, Bedford C5Z1 PUT 659 with Duple Super Vista bodywork was delivered to Ibstock garage, similar vehicle PUT 660 was operated by Markfield. Photo/ R H G Simpson

a nothing short of a saviour for many small independent operators. Many of the vehicles purchased had only recently undergone major overhauls at Aldernham Works.

Birds (dealers) of Stratford purchased large numbers of RTs and these were resold to operators throughout the country. Browns Blue were regular customers of Birds and took advantage of the RTs availability by purchasing nine examples in total. RTs began to appear at Markfield depot in May and arrived in a steady trickle until the last vehicle arrived in November 1958. The first to arrive was former RT 173 HLW 160 with Park Royal bodywork; this was the only Brown's Blue RT to not be fitted with a roof number box. This was followed by former RT 410 and 420 HLX 227 and HLX 237 respectively, both carrying Weymann bodywork. Next came former RT 179 and 164 HLW 166 and HLW 151 respectively, both carrying Park Royal bodywork. Also in September former RT 408 HLX 225, with Weymann body was purchased. In October former RTs 157 and 419 HLW 144 and HLX 236 were delivered carrying Park Royal and Weymann bodywork respectively. The final RT to arrive was former RT 272 HLX 89 with Park Royal bodywork.

I can remember visiting the Flying Horse public house with my parents on a summer Sunday evening, (it was then and still is adjacent to the Markfield depot) and we sat in the rear garden. I was probably enjoying a bottle of Vimto and a bag of flavoured crisps, a new phenomenon in those days. I recall noticing a line of red double deckers standing to the right of the yard. Some looked a little unkempt with their paper side adverts in shreds and peeling off, but it wouldn't be long before a nice coat of deep blue paint relieved with red would smarten their appearance.

The AEC Regent RT. These vehicles were the mainstay of the London Transport fleet from the post–war period through to the late fifties. Large scale withdrawals of the class were brought about by the introduction of the Routemaster. Many operators in this country and overseas snapped up these popular vehicles to modernise their own fleets. RT 410 is seen here in central London on the 8th May 1951, it later entered the Browns Blue fleet in July 1958. **Photo/ Alan B Cross**

Enter the RT era, formally RT 420 HLX 237 dating from 1947. It is seen here on 21st June 1958 parked on the ramp at Markfield awaiting preparation for service during the summer of 1958, with two unidentified RT's alongside. They were part of the first batch of five similar vehicles purchased in June 1958. They still bear LT livery. HLX 237 entered service in July 1958 and was fitted with platform doors during September of that year. **Photo/ Richard Butler**

Taken on the same day former LT (RT 164) HLW 151 with Park Royal bodywork awaits preparation for service at Markfield. Platform doors were fitted before entering service on 1st September 1958, other modifications included the removal of the side and rear destination boxes, which were panelled over. HLW 151 was the last vehicle to operate in Browns Blue service. **Photo/ Richard Butler**

This rear view of Weymann bodied HLX 227 formally RT 410 shows clearly the fitment of an emergency door, part of the construction and use regulations required for a certificate of fitness, when platform doors are fitted, HLX 227 also entered service on 1st September 1958. **Photo/ R. H. G. Simpson**

Odd man out amongst the aquired RTs was Park Royal bodied HLW 160 formally RT 173. This was actually the first RT to enter service. It was the only vehicle not fitted with a roof box, possibly the result of the complex overhaul system in place at London Transports Aldenham Works, RTs entered the works, the chassis and body were separated, the chassis generally took just over a week to refurbish, but the body took considerably longer. The chassis and body were never reunited, resulting in some "Mix and Match" oddities within the RTclass. It is seen here on a wet day in Bagworth working the Coalville to Hinckley service. **Photo/ Roy Marshall**

HLX 237 formally RT 420 with Weymann bodywork is seen making its way along the A50 after leaving Markfield bound for Whitwick. **Photo/ Mark K. Swallow**

Seen standing on the forecourt of the Nelson café on the corner of Ratby Lane, Field Head, HLW 166 formally RT 179 awaits its next journey. The "ESSO" sign of Warners garage can just be seen in the background. This vehicle was withdrawn prematurely in February 1963 after a serious accident badly damaged the rear of the Park Royal bodywork. **Photo/ Robert F Mack**

Taken on a wet day near to the Ellistown Hotel, HLW 151 formally RT 164 makes its way to Ibstock. All of the RTs later received modified front destination boxes in the early sixties. **Photo/ Photobus**

About to make the long journey to Measham, RT408 HLX 225 is seen in St. Margaret's Bus Station, Leicester. Just visible on the left is Dennis rebuild EAY 58. **Photo/ Photobus**

About to enter the Leicester City boundary at Glenfield Frith Drive, HLW 144 formally RT 157 picks up passengers. Competition was intense between various local operators on this section of route into Leicester. **Photo/ Alan B Cross**

This atmospheric photograph was taken from inside the old concrete bus shelters at St. Margaret's Bus Station, HLX 236 formally RT 419 with Weymann bodywork stands alongside a BMMO D5 or D5B receiving some mechanical attention.
Photo/ Mike Sutcliffe MBE

Most of the ex-London RTs were fitted with platform doors prior to entering service, there were however two, possibly three exceptions. HLW 160 and HLX 237 both entered service without doors, but they were fitted by October 1958. However there is a mystery surrounding HLW 166, it may also have received doors later in the year. Although most major body repairs were carried out at Markfield, RT platform doors were made up and fitted at Ibstock Garage under the watchful eye of Garage Foreman Roy Briers. A company called Redco of Beverley (later to become Deans) in east Yorkshire was manufacturing rear platform doors in kit form to fit the ex-LT RTs. One kit was purchased by Browns to analyse measurements and the method of construction, thereafter Roy built all of the remaining units himself and they were all fitted at Ibstock.

To compensate for this large influx of vehicles several coaches and four of the Daimlers were withdrawn. The first to go in April was Bedford OB EJU 786 it was sold for use as a mobile shop. In May the last of the Tilling Stevens ENR 792 was sold for scrap, in June it was Daimler GLX 905, followed by the ex-Southport Daimler EWM 372 in July. August saw ex-London Transport HGC 288 withdrawn and the former Maidstone and District Leyland TD7 GKL 765. In October ex-London Transport GYE 64 was taken out of service. All of these vehicles were sold to Birds of Stratford (dealer) for scrap, and finally the Foden FVSC6 FJU 533 was withdrawn in November, bringing about the largest transformation in one year of the fleet so far.

On 1st July 1958 a timetable booklet was produced at a price of 3d giving full information about all stage carriage services

The last of the RT's to be purchased was Park Royal bodied HLX 89 formally RT 272 which entered service without platform doors in December 1958. It is seen here entering Gravel Street from Lower Church Gate, Leicester shortly after entering service. It was finally fitted with platform doors in September 1959. Photo/ Mike Sutcliffe MBE

operated from both Markfield and Ibstock garages. Previously separate timetables had been available for each garage. Longer distance tours and excursions were also advertised.

There was something of a lull in vehicle activity in the first half of 1959. Former LT Daimler HGF 806, which had been heavily rebuilt was withdrawn in February and sent to Birds for scrap. In September the Leyland TS8 BNR 59 was taken out of service, also in September and October the final two ex-LT Daimlers HGC 296 and HGC 292 were withdrawn, both going to Birds, Stratford (dealer) for scrap,. During the last few months

Taken towards the end of its service with Browns Blue, Daimler HGC 292 loads for a journey to Stanton-u-Bardon. This was the last of the former LT Daimlers to be withdrawn from service, in October 1959. **Photo/ John Allan Collection**

Taken at the Birds premises in Stratford upon Avon, Daimler GLX 905 sadly awaits the cutting torch with GKL 765 to the right. **Photo/ Unknown**

Also seen at the same time at Birds and awaiting the same fate, is the former Maidstone and District Leyland TD7 with Weymann bodywork. Both vehicles were withdrawn by Browns during the summer of 1958. Photo/ Unknown

in service, these two vehicles spent most of their time on contracts, stadium and football specials or the Desford Colliery Village service. The former Parson Dennis Lancet III FUT 777 was withdrawn in November and the ex-Hill Bedford OWB DRY 777 was withdrawn in December and sold for a mobile shop.

Vehicles entering the fleet commenced with a second hand AEC Reliance VTB 320 with Plaxton Venturer bodywork dating from 1955. An acquisition which on the face of it seemed a little surprising was that of a former Leicester AEC Regent II DJF 323 with Weymann bodywork, a far cry from the recently purchased ex-LT AEC Regent RT's. Its crash gearbox proved to be useful for driver training and it also replaced the ex-LT Daimlers on the Desford Colliery Village service and was a regular performer on the Coalville to Ibstock service. It worked from Ibstock garage for most of its time with Browns. Another second hand AEC Reliance

Although the double deck acquisitions tended to overshadow vehicle movements, several second hand coach purchases took place at this time. VTB 320 an AEC Reliance with Plaxton Venturer bodywork was purchased in September 1959. Photo/ Roy Marshall

Former Parsons Dennis Lancet III, FUT 777 appears to be bogged down in a field. It is seen after it had passed to its new owner, Truelove of Bradford, for non-psv use. Photo/ J. C. Collin

4328 UA also entered service at this time, Duple Britannia bodywork was fitted, followed by two older AEC Regal IIIs EF 8927 and EF 8928, both carrying Plaxton Venturer bodywork.

Parked in Groby village, EF 8928 an AEC Regal III with Plaxton Venturer bodywork. It was one of two similar vehicles purchased from Bee-line, West Hartlepool. Photo/ R. F. Mack

After some experiments a new coach livery was adopted in 1959. Some side flashes and window surrounds had been painted in primrose for several years, although there was no standardisation in this. Eventually two shades of a lighter blue were adopted and this would become standard for all coaches from this point onwards with the more modern fully fronted coaches carrying the new scheme well. The remaining half cab coaches that were repainted, did to my mind, look a little uneasy in their new livery. All double deck vehicles retained the deeper blue and red colour scheme in use since their revamp in the mid-1950s.

Due to the large increases in private car ownership nationwide, it was no secret that bus passenger numbers had been in decline since the mid- fifties, a situation that had been of constant concern to the bus industry. Duplication of routes by one or more operators was looked upon as a negative policy; consolidation was needed if services and indeed operators were to survive.

Former Leicester City Transport AEC Regent II, DJF 323 with Weymann bodywork, was purchased in October 1959. It spent most of its life with Browns at Ibstock garage. **Photo/ Ken Jubb**

Midland Red was the major operator in Leicestershire and it had steadily expanded its route network in the county by purchasing several smaller private operators during the mid-fifties, companies such as Allens of Mountsorrel, Boyers of Rothley and Kemp and Shaw of Leicester were all purchased. In some instances vehicles passed to Midland Red and were to be operated for some years. St. Margaret's Bus Station was a mecca for enthusiasts who liked to see traditional BMMO built vehicles rubbing shoulders with vehicles manufactured elsewhere, all under the same ownership.

In west Leicestershire two larger operators Gibsons (Comfort) of Barlestone and Browns Blue Coaches Ltd were still thriving, running very well established services to a variety of destinations protected by long standing agreements to operate the services they had without "stepping on the toes" of the other operators. This worked very well in general with the exception of the section of the A50 from Leicester (Groby Road) to Glenfield Turn, a road junction five miles to the west of the City. No less than four operators competed for this lucrative section of route. Two Inspectors were employed to "keep an eye" on the route network and to make adjustments when the need arose. George Brown (Laurie's brother) looked after the Markfield section spending much of his time in and around St. Margaret's Bus Station, whilst George Holmes was responsible for the Ibstock routes, although he travelled all over the route network ticket checking.

Northern Coachbuilders bodied AEC Regent III KWB 82 was a former Sheffield vehicle. It was one of a pair purchased in June 1960 and it is seen here at Ibstock working the Coalville to Hinckley service.
Photo/ Roy Marshall

Some Saturday and all Sunday services operating the Leicester to Whitwick and Leicester to Ibstock routes were altered at this time. The Leicester to Stanton-u-Bardon service was discontinued and replaced by the two main routes. All buses now called at Stanton-u-Bardon this was achieved by turning round at the bottom of the village, reversing at the Crown Inn public house before retracing the route back to the main A50. The Whitwick service would then carry on its normal route, however the Ibstock service would travel via Bardon Chapel and Ellistown onto Ibstock, at this point the route was extended via Heather, Packington, or Swepstone (Sats) to either Ashby or Measham (Sats). This allowed the Ibstock to Ashby service operated on Sundays to be withdrawn. This route was normally worked by a coach.

Ibstock drivers were not too happy with these alterations, the roads between Heather and Ashby were winding and narrow, not really suitable for double deck vehicles where overhanging trees were also a problem, but these alterations remained in place until the takeover.

In order to maintain its share of services Browns Blue was upgrading its fleet by making second-hand purchases during 1960. A total of six vehicles were acquired all of AEC manufacture. Two former Sheffield AEC Regent III double deckers KWB 82 and KWB 85 with Northern Coachbuilders bodywork, and three AEC Reliance coaches with Duple Britannia bodywork, LWH 3, MWH 4 and MWH 5 respectively, all came from Hargreaves of Bolton. They were followed by another AEC Regent III double decker OFC 403 featuring a normal "crash" type gearbox, with Weymann bodywork, this time from City of Oxford Motor Services.

However no fewer than twelve vehicles were withdrawn in that year. In January two of the once numerous Dennis coaches AAY 6 and JU 5854 were taken out of service. They had both been re-bodied with Yeates coach

The other ex-Sheffield Regent, KWB 85 is seen here leaving Hinckley, near Sunnyside Hospital bound for Coalville. Photo/ R. F. Mack

Formally City of Oxford, a 1949 AEC Regent III OFC 403, with Weymann bodywork is pictured here in Ibstock (High Street). **Photo/ Ken jubb**

Three second hand AEC Reliance MU3RV coaches purchased from Hargreaves of Bolton entered the fleet in September 1960, two with Duple Britannia bodywork, and one with Plaxton Venturer bodywork which is seen here still with its original owner. **Photo/ R.H.G. Simpson**

LWH 3 stands in St. Margaret's Bus Station, Leicester. It received the revised coach livery being applied to Browns coaches at that time when it entered service.
Photo/ John Clark Collection

bodies and fitted with AEC 7.7 litre engines during 1955. The bodies were fitted to EAY 58 and EJU 260 both of which were Dennis Lancets III. No less than nine vehicles were withdrawn in September, one double decker EJU 541 the first of the Brush bodied Daimlers delivered new in 1947, one Dennis Lancet with Duple bodywork FUT 452, plus four AEC coaches, two Regal half cabs ADO 619, KAL 99 and two Regal IVs with Yeates bodywork GUT 398 and GUT 400. The remaining three were all Leyland Tigers, two with rare Wilkes and Meade bodywork KUG 6 and KUM 521, and one half cab with Yeates body EAY 180. Finally the ex-demonstrator Daimler CD650 KHP998, with Roe bodywork was taken out of service in December. Unfortunately this rare vehicle was scrapped

A single purchase during 1961 was in some ways unusual, this being another AEC Regent III HTT 333, but of the 3RT type which came from Devon General. It could be said that in the interests of standardisation an ex-LT RT

The third AEC Reliance, purchased from Hargeaves of Bolton was MWH 5 bodied by Duple is seen here on private hire duties in Blackpool. Photo/ Roy Marshall

During the autumn of 1959 it was decided to replace the two Dennis Lancet chassis belonging to the two Dennis rebuilds completed during 1955. AAY 6 was the first vehicle to receive a second hand chassis from Dennis Lancet III EAY 58 in January 1960. It is seen here in St. Margaret's Bus Station after a heavy snow shower (above).

The second Dennis rebuild was dealt with in February 1960, Dennis Lancet III EJU 260 was the donor vehicle in this case (below). Both of the Dennis Lancet II chassis were scrapped. **Photos/ Derek Westall**

The "light up" is probably the only source of heat for the crew of former City of Oxford AEC Regent III OFC 403, it awaits the prospect of a cold, bleak journey "over the top" to Whitwick. **Photo/ Derek Westall**

AEC Reliance VTB 320 looks a little tired as it nears the end of its days with Browns Blue, however this vehicle passed to local operator Staplefords of Markfield for many years of further service. **Photo/ Derek Westall**

Another AEC Regent III HTT 333, this time an RT type entered the fleet during September 1961, surprisingly not aquired from the London fleet, but coming from Devon General. Provincial style bodywork by Weymann was fitted; it is seen here at Ibstock garage. **Photo/ C.W. Ruuth**

The final two new vehicles to be purchased in June 1962 were both Bedford SB5s with Harrington Crusader bodywork, registration numbers 726/727 AUT. 727 AUT is pictured here on private hire duties. **Photo/ R.H.G. Simpson**

Taken shortly after entering service during July 1962, former Devon General AEC Regent III KOD 592 with Weymann bodywork stands in St. Margaret's Bus Station, Leicester. KOD 592 would only spend seven months in the Brown fleet before for passing to local operator Gibson of Barlestone. Photo/ Mike Sutcliffe

would have been the preferred choice, but as can be seen from the fleet lists, total standardisation was not a priority.

The penultimate Bedford OB ENR 294 was sold in October 1961 for use as a Mobile Shop and in November of the same year the second of the Brush bodied Daimlers FAY 517 was sold for scrap.

A brief look through the fare charts for July 1962 reveals that an adult single fare from Leicester to Whitwick would cost 2s/4d, travelling from Hinckley to Newbold Verdon would cost an adult 1s/8d, a miner living in Ibstock travelling to Whitwick Colliery would pay 10d, and the adult fare from Leicester to Measham was 2s/11d. Football supporters would pay 2s/5d single fare from Heather to Leicester City Football Ground and Speedway fans would pay 2s/1d single fare from Ellistown.

It is also interesting to note that passengers could be carried within the area stop signs in Leicester. A protective fare system charging substantially higher fares than on the L.C.T. services had been in operation for some time. These fares were designed to discourage intending passengers from using these services and succeeded to a large degree.

Two new additions to the coaching fleet during June 1962 were Bedford SB5s 726 AUT and 727 AUT, both with Harrington bodywork. These were to be the last new vehicles supplied and were only in service for just over eight months. The final addition to the fleet was another AEC Regent III KOD 592, with Weymann purchased in July 1962, formally a Devon General vehicle. As in the past rear platform doors were fitted before entering service. These vehicles replaced Bedford SB JNR 926 with Yeates Riviera bodywork which was scrapped. Dennis Lancet III FUT 527 with Duple bodywork, which brought about the final withdrawal of a half cab coach in the fleet and AEC Regent II DJF 323 the ex-Leicester Weymann bodied double decker which was sold for use as a caravan, the last Bedford OB with Duple Vista bodywork FUT 339, and finally the Leyland PS1/1 KUG 3, an ex-Wallace Arnold coach with Duple FC33F bodywork, it was withdrawn in November 1962 and sold to former driver Les Hanagan. Included in the arrangement was the overnight contract to the Bristol Siddely Aero Engine factory at Ansty, near Coventry, operated on behalf of the PSV Ltd. With the help of another part time PSV driver who conveniently also worked at the factory, Les was able to park the coach up overnight in Coventry, returning in the morning thus saving dead mileage. School contracts were carried out during the day by Les.

An unfortunate accident which occurred on the A50 at the top of Markfield village in the late Autumn of 1962 involved ex-LT RT HLW 166. Ironically a former Browns Blue Dennis rebuild which now belonged to Forsell, a dyeing company from Wigston, Leicester was working an employee's special when it skidded on a patch of black ice running into the rear of the stationary RT which was standing at a bus stop. Damage to the platform area and stairs was considerable; the bus was taken back to Markfield garage, but never repaired.

Although after many months of rumour and speculation concerning a possible takeover by the Midland Red, it was nonetheless a little surprising to hear that an agreement had been reached between the two companies. The Coalville Times made the announcement on the front page of its 9th November 1962 edition, the headlines read;

BROWNS BLUE TO BE TAKEN OVER BY MIDLAND RED

The next stage was for the Midland Red to apply to the East Midland Traffic Commissioners to take over the services and to make any alterations deemed necessary to continue with operations. If approved the final takeover would be early in the New Year, in retrospect a little optimistic bearing in mind what was about to prove a very difficult time for all involved. Sixty five platform staff were expected to be offered further employment, however maintenance staff and office workers would not be offered jobs.

The Chairman and joint Managing Director of the company Mr Reg Brown told the newspaper that they had as yet no plans for the future and that all vehicles would be sold on by the family as public service vehicles. Only the Shaw Lane depot at Markfield would pass into Midland Red hands.

A short article in the 14th December edition of the local newspaper mentioned that a spokesman from Browns Blue had said that a "merger" may be possible in early February 1963, unfortunately this was a little premature as serious negotiations were still taking place. As the new year passed negotiations between Browns Blue, the Midland Red and The Traffic Commissioners were reaching a critical stage and none of the parties could afford any distractions. However, the winter of 1962/63 was almost certainly the worst on record since the terrible winter of 1947, from December through to February the whole country endured sub-zero temperatures twenty four hours a day, also heavy snowfalls, strong winds and blizzards which had a very serious affect on public transport in all parts of the country.

Many communities were cut off by drifting snow for days, in some cases weeks. Services in Leicestershire were badly affected; the bus companies carried on as best they could but on the night of Saturday 19th January 1963 attempts to maintain the Leicester to Whitwick service were abruptly halted at 6 p.m. The 5.05pm ex-Leicester to Whitwick service driven by Jack Clark was making its way from Copt Oak towards Abbotts Oak when a small van became stuck on Irish Hill near Copt Oak, the highest point in Leicestershire. This area is very exposed and heavy blizzards with almost zero visibility hampered the vehicles recovery. Soon traffic began to pile up behind it including, unfortunately, a Browns Blue double decker bus.

Work carried on and eventually all other vehicles were rescued but the bus by now was engulfed by snow. Arrangements were made to take the passengers away. A team of Police Officers attempted to dig the bus out, even a tow was unsuccessful and after four hours all hope was abandoned. The bus remained there until Sunday morning when a group of Browns Blue employees plus some workers from Bardon Hill Quarry, went up to Irish Hill. They also brought a 150hp digger to cut a single passage through six foot snow drifts. When they eventually reached the bus it was an amazing sight that greeted them, the snow had drifted up to the bottom of the upper deck windows on the offside. In a statement to the press Mr Norman Brown said "that the van was the cause of the blockage, the bus and several other vehicles had then unfortunately become trapped".

A month later the Coalville Times finally confirmed the news in its 22nd February 1963 edition that Browns Blue Coaches Ltd would be sold to the Midland Red.

I quote from the headlines and front page:-

BROWNS BLUE SERVICES WILL END ON MARCH 15TH

MIDLAND RED - TAKEOVER IS FINALLY SETTLED

Browns Blue buses will go into service for the last time on Friday March 15th. The company's services will be operated the following day by the Midland Red.

The takeover of Browns services follows months of negotiation, which were completed at a Transport Commissioners' public sitting at the weekend, when the remaining few services were turned over to the Midland Red.

The routes will be basically the same as operated by Browns Blue Coaches Ltd. In some cases, buses on the Whitwick to Leicester route will travel via Hall Lane and Greenhill Estate instead of Copt Oak.

IBSTOCK SERVICES

At the Transport Commissioners sitting, Midland Red successfully applied for the Leicester to Ibstock services after they had agreed with a request from Ibstock Parish Council to run buses at 7.10a.m.and 5.40p.m. for work people, and one from Ibstock at 1.15p.m. on Wednesdays for shopkeepers who wished to visit Leicester.

An application for a slight deviation of the route operated by Browns Blue was turned down after being opposed by the County Council.

The route from Leicester was now to be operated via Markfield and Stanton, and instead of continuing to Battleflat, it would double back to the main A50 and Bardon Chapel, Ellistown and Ibstock.

The Council stated that the road from Stanton to Battleflat was not suitable for an increased volume of traffic.

UNRESTRICTED

Midland Red traffic manager Mr R. Brandon, said Browns buses were using that particular stretch of road, which was better than many roads in the county carrying heavy traffic.

Mr Reginald Lawrence Brown, of Browns Blue Coaches Ltd said the road was completely unrestricted and 69 buses were using the road each week.

The Midland Red divisional superintendent, Mr D. M. Kirby, said there was a quarter to half a mile vision on the majority of the road.

The company anticipated taking about 262 buses along the road each week. Submitting a report of the road statistics, the county council said the road was narrow in places and when two large vehicles met, one had to mount the grass verge.

COST £11,500

"An increased volume of traffic would create a dangerous situation" they said. The council agreed with Mr Brandon that the extra services would mean only one bus an hour passing along the road.

The council's area surveyor Mr J. H. Scarlett said he had examined the road and had prepared an estimate for improvement and widening. It would cost about £11,500 Mr Scarlett said, it was doubtful whether the County Highways Committee would agree to such a scheme.

Turning down the application the Minister's Inspector said it seemed that the Midland Red wished to use the road to save mileage.

"A lot of heavy traffic will be using this road when the M1 reaches the area and we do not feel justified in authorising additional bus services", he added. ***COALVILLE TIMES***

There were several other details to be considered. Browns Blue operated a variety of school contracts using Term Contract Tickets, from both Markfield Garage (to Forest Rock Grammar School 200 scholars) and on varying routes from Ibstock garages (85-90 scholars). Also many children in the area were issued with travel passes to be used on normal stage carriage services. A total of the numbers involved as well as the financial aspect would need to be accounted for, the Midland Red notified the Education Authority that it would be preferable for all scholars to be issued with Midland Red passes starting on the day of the takeover. Many of these arrangements were already in place on Midland Red services making the changeover quite straightforward. It was likely that the takeover would take place mid-way through the school term, therefore it would be important to finalise matters well in advance of this day.

Colliery and workers contracts were also a major part of Browns Blue operations, some colliery services would be integrated into the Midland Red service network, others were to be taken over by the newly formed Reliant Coaches of Ibstock and Staplefords of Markfield. Workers contracts covered many routes within the Coalville and Leicester areas such as English Electric at Whetstone; these were rearranged through the PSV Ltd in Leicester.

Obviously the sale of Browns Blue was not quite so straight forward as it would seem.

Browns Blue Coaches Ltd

Stage Carriage Route Network Circa 1958-60

School and works contracts were also operated throughout Leicestershire and into Coventry, Warwickshire.

Chapter VIII

Ticket Machines, Fares, Timetables and Parcels

TICKET MACHINES

It is not certain what type of tickets were used on the first services from Stanton-u-Bardon to Anstey, but as more routes to Whitwick, Leicester and Loughborough were introduced pre-printed Bell Punch tickets were introduced. The Bell Punch system remained in use until approximately 1955 when local operator C. H. Allen of Mountsorrel sold its business to the Midland Red; this included the associate business of Kemp and Shaw. Thirty Setright types C-LR. D pattern machines were in use at that time and were numbered A1 through to A30. Browns Blue purchased a number of these machines from C. H. Allen putting them to use at the Ibstock garage.

Markfield garage also used these machines, but retained some of the original Bell Punch system until about 1960/61, when they

Ticket machine and equipment with the kind permission of Pauline and Lloyd Burton

progressed onto the Setright Insert machine. About a year later Ibstock placed its first Setright Speed machine into service, followed by several more a short time later. These proved to be very useful on the busy Coalville to Ibstock route.

Transport Historian Allan T Condie has collated detailed information from the Setright sales book It shows that Browns Blue purchased its first Setright Speed SMB machines in November 1958 numbered BB1-2, BB3-4 followed in July 1959 and single purchase of BB5 came in December 1959. During August and October 1961 machine numbers BB6-7, and BB8-9 were purchased respectively, finally machines BB10-11 were supplied in October 1962.

Tickets issued by Browns Blue were only accepted on Browns services, there were no reciprocal arrangements made with any other operators for the interchange of tickets, Ten Trip Tickets or Day Returns etc.

FARES

On routes shared with other operators, the fares were generally agreed between each operator under the watchful eye of the Traffic Commissioners. Fare Stages were agreed and adhered to, although the main competitor. The Midland Red often favoured multiple fare stages within the boundaries of some towns and villages. Browns tried to simplify the system by charging an overall fare for the same distance travelled within a town or village boundary, but after a short time the Midland Red became aware of this because passenger loadings were favouring Browns within local boundaries. Inevitably after complaints by the Midland Red to the Traffic Commissioners, alterations were made by Browns which led to small value tickets being added to these fares to bring them into line.

At the end of each shift, conductors working from Ibstock would complete their waybill and place all takings into a drop safe at Reg Brown's house which was opposite the garage in Leicester Road, Ibstock. The Markfield platform staff would take their takings to the original house in Ashby Road, where the company first began. Depot Manager Jack Neill, now living there, was responsible for all cash paid in.

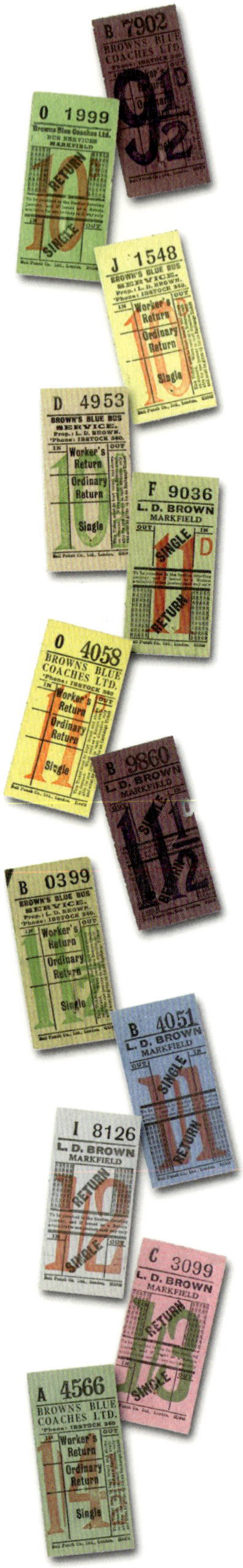

BROWN'S BLUE Bus Service

(Late Pride of Stanton Service)

L. D. BROWN, Proprietor Markfield.

TELEPHONE : MARKFIELD 14.

TIME TABLE to run between LEICESTER (All Saint's Road) and STANTON-under-BARDON.

Route : All Saint's Road, via Great Central Street, Groby Road, Markfield, Shaw Lane.

MONDAYS, TUESDAYS, THURSDAYS, FRIDAYS

			a.m.	a.m.	a.m.	a.m.	p.m.	p.m.	*	p.m.
LEICESTER A.S. Rd.	dep.	-	7.5	8.0	8.15	9.25	6.0	6.25	6.35	7.15
GROBY	app.	-	7.20	8.15	8.30	9.40	6.15	6.40	6.50	7.30
MARKFIELD Q. Head	,,	-	7.30	8.25	8.40	9.50	6.25	6.50	7.0	7.40
CLIFFE HILL	,,	-					6 30			7.45
STANTON	arr.	-					6.35		7.10	7.50

			a.m.	*	a.m.	a.m.	a.m.	p.m.
STANTON	dep.	-		7.5	7.15		8.0	5.0
CLIFFE HILL	app.	-			7.20		8.5	5.5
MARKFIELD Q. Head	,,	-	6.10	7.15	7.25	7.30	8.10	5.10
GROBY	,,	-	6.20	7.25	7.35	7.40	8.20	5.20
LEICESTER A.S. Rd.	arr.	-	6.35	7.40	7.50	7.55	8.35	6.35

WEDNESDAYS

			a.m.	a.m.	a.m.	a.m.	p.m.	p.m.	p.m.	*	p.m.	p.m.	p.m.
LEICESTER A.S. Rd.	dep.	-	7.5	8.0	8.15	11.5	3.35	6.0	6.25	6.35	7.15	10.30	10.50
GROBY	app.	-	7.20	8.15	8.30	11.20	3.50	6.15	6.40	6.50	7.30	10.45	11.5
MARKFIELD Q. Head	,,	-	7.30	8.25	8.40	11.30	4.0	6.25	6.50	7.0	7.40	10.55	11.15
CLIFFE HILL	,,	-				11.35	4.5	6 30			7.45	11.0	
STANTON	arr.	-				11.40	4.10	6.35		7.10	7.50	11.5	

			a.m.	*	a.m.	a.m.	a.m.	a.m.	p.m.	p.m.	p.m.
STANTON	dep.	-		7.5	7.15		8.0	9.30	2.0	5.0	8.0
CLIFFE HILL	app.	-			7.20		8.5	9.35	2.5	5.5	8.5
MARKFIELD Q. Head	,,	-	6.10	7.15	7.25	7.30	8.10	9.40	2.10	5.10	8.10
GROBY	,,	-	6.20	7.25	7.35	7.40	8.20	9.50	2.20	5.20	8.20
LEICESTER A.S. Road	arr.	.	6.35	7.40	7.50	7.55	8.35	10.5	2.35	5.35	8.35

SATURDAYS

		a.m.	a.m.	a.m.	a.m.	p.m.	p.m.	p.m.	p.m.	p.m.	p.m.	p.m.	p.m.	p.m.
LEICESTER	dep.	7.5	8.0	8.15	11.5	12.25	1.0	3.5	3.40	4.25	6.10	8.5	10.5	10.50
GROBY	app.	7.20	8.15	8.30	11.20	12.40	1.15	3.20	3.55	4.40	6.25	8.20	10.20	11.5
MARKFIELD	,,	7.30	8.25	8.40	11.30	12.50	1.25	3.30	4.5	4.50	6.35	8.30	10.30	11.15
CLIFFE HILL	,,					12.55	1.30	3.35		4.55	6.40	8.35	10.35	
STANTON	arr.					1.0	1.35	3.40		5.0	6.45	8.40	10.40	

		a.m.	*	a.m.	a.m.	a.m.	a.m.	p.m.	p.m.	p.m.	p.m.	p.m.	p.m.	p.m.
STANTON	dep.		7.5	7.15		8.0	9.30	2.0	2.50	4.30	5.0	7.10	9.0	10.0
CLIFFE HILL	app.			7.20		8.5	9.35	2.5	2.55	4.35	5.5	7.15	9.5	10.5
MARKFIELD	,,	6.10	7.15	7.25	7.30	8.10	9.40	2.10	3.0	4.40	5.10	7.20	9.10	10.10
GROBY	,,	6.20	7.25	7.35	7.40	8.20	9.50	2.20	3.10	4.50	5.20	7.30	9.20	10.20
LEICESTER	arr.	6.35	7.40	7.50	7.55	8.35	10.5	2.35	3.25	5.5	5.35	7.45	9.35	10.35

SUNDAYS

	a.m.	p.m.	p.m.	p.m.
LEICESTER	10.50	3.10	10.5	10.45
GROBY	11.5	3.25	10.20	11.0
MARKFIELD	11.15	3.35	10.30	11.10
CLIFFE HILL	11.20	3.40	10.35	
STANTON	11.25	3.45	10.40	

	a.m.	a.m.	p.m.	p.m.	p.m.	p.m.	p.m.
STANTON		9.30		1.45	8.30	9.25	
CLIFFE HILL		9.35		1.50	8.35	9.30	
MARKFIELD	8.50	9.40	1.30	1.55	8.40	9.35	10.0
GROBY	9.0	9.50	1.40	2.5	8.50	9.45	10.10
LEICESTER	9.15	10.5	1.55	2.20	9.5	10.0	10.25

* These 'buses run via Shaw Lane.

BOOK ONE OF BROWN'S BLUE . . SALOONS FOR YOUR PRIVATE PARTY

Charnwood Publishing Co., Coalville, Leicester.

Timetable circa 1936 for the Leicester to Stanton-under-Bardon service

BROWN'S BLUE Bus Service

JAN. 1st, 1936.

L. D. BROWN (Proprietor) : Markfield.

Telephone : Markfield 214.

TIME TABLE to run between LEICESTER (All Saints' Rd.) and WHITWICK (Market Place).

Route : Via Groby, Markfield, Shaw Lane, Copt Oak, Greenhill and Forest Rock

SUNDAYS.

	a.m.	a.m.	p.m.	p.m.	p.m.	p.m.	p.m.
LEICESTER (A.S. Rd.) dep.	9.20	11.5	2.5	3.40	6.25	8.10	9.50
GROBY app. „	9.35	11.20	2.20	3.55	6.40	8.25	10.5
MARKFIELD (Green) „	9.45	11.30	2.25	4.5	6.50	8.30	10.15
MARKFIELD (Q. Head) „	9.48	11.33	2.28	4.8	6.53	8.33	10.18
SHAW LANE „	9.51	11.36	2.31	4.11	6.56	8.36	10.21
COPT OAK „	9.53	11.38	2.33	4.13	6.58	8.38	10.23
GREENHILL „	9.58	11.43	2.38	4 18	7.3	8.43	10.28
FOREST ROCK „	10.3	11.48	2.43	4.23	7.8	8.48	10.33
WHITWICK app. arrives	10.8	11.53	2.48	4.28	7.13	8.53	10.38

	a.m.	p.m.	p.m.	p.m.	p.m.	p.m.	p.m.
WHITWICK app. departs	10.15	2.50	5.20	7.15	8.55	9 45	10.40
FOREST ROCK „	10.20	2.55	5.25	7.20	9.0	9.50	10.45
GREENHILL „	10.23	2.58	5.28	7.23	9.5	9.55	10.48
COPT OAK „	10.28	3.3	5.33	7.28	9.10	10.0	10.53
SHAW LANE „	10.30	3.5	5.35	7.30	9.12	10.2	10.55
MARKFIELD (Green) „	10.33	3.8	5.38	7.33		10.5	10 58
MARKFIELD (Q. Head)„	10.35	3.10	5.40	7.35	9.15	10.8	
GROBY „	10.45	3.15	5.50	7.45	9.25	10.15	
LEICESTER (A.S. Rd.) arr.	11.0	3.30	6.5	8.0	9.40	10.30	

WEDNESDAYS.

	a.m.	p.m.	p.m.	p.m.	p.m.	p m.
LEICESTER (A.S. Rd.) dep.	9.25	12.30	2.15	4.50	7.15	9.20
GROBY app. „	9.40	12.45	2.30	5.5	7.30	9.35
MARKFIELD (Green) „	9.50	12.55	2.40	5.15	7.40	9.40
MARKFIELD (Q. Head) „	9.53	12.58	2.43	5.18	7.43	9.43
SHAW LANE „	9.56	1.1	2.46	5.21	7.46	9.46
COPT OAK „	9.58	1.3	2.48	5.23	7.48	9.48
GREENHILL „	10.3	1.8	2.53	5.28	7.53	9 53
FOREST ROCK „	10.8	1.13	2.58	5.33	7.58	9.58
WHITWICK arrives	10.13	1.18	3.3	5.38	8.3	10.3

	a.m.	a.m.	p.m.	p.m.	p.m.	p.m.	p.m.	p.m.
WHITWICK departs	9.20	10.20	1.20	2.15	3.20	5.45	8.10	10.5
FOREST ROCK app. „	9.25	10.25	1.25	2 20	3.25	5.50	8.15	10.10
GREENHILL „	9.30	10.28	1.28	2.25	3.30	5.55	8.18	10.15
COPT OAK „	9.35	10.33	1.33	2.30	3.35	6.0	8.23	10.20
SHAW LANE „	9.37	10.35	1.35	2.32	3.37	6.2	8.25	10.22
MARKFIELD (Green) „		10.38	1.38				8.28	
MARKFIELD (Q. Head) „	9.40	10.40	1.40	2.35	3.40	6.5	8.30	10.25
GROBY „	9.50	10.50	1.50	2.45	3.50	6.15	8.40	10.30
LEICESTER (A.S. Rd.) arr.	10.5	11.5	2.5	3.0	4.5	6.30	8.55	10.45

SATURDAYS. & Holiday Monday & Tuesday

	a.m	p.m	p.m	p.m	p.m	p.m	p.m	p.m
LEICESTER (A.S. Rd.) dep.	9.25	12.25	2.15	4.50	6.0	7.20	9.20	10.50
GROBY app „	9.40	12.40	2.30	5.5	6.15	7.35	9.35	11.5
MARKFIELD (Green) „	9.50	12.50	2.40	5.15	6.25	7.45	9.40	11.15
MARKFIELD (Q. Head) „	9.53	12.53	2.43	5.18	6.28	7.48	9.43	11.17
SHAW LANE „	9.56	12.56	2.46	5.21	6.31	7.51	9.46	11.20
COPT OAK „	9.58	12.58	2.48	5.23	6,33	7.53	9.48	11.22
GREENHILL „	10.3	1.3	2.53	5.28	6.38	7,58	9.53	11,27
FOREST ROCK „	10.8	1.8	2.58	5.33	6.43	8.3	9,58	11.32
WHITWICK arrives	10,13	1.13	3.3	5.38	6,48	8.8	10.3	11.37

	a.m	a.m	a.m	p.m	p.m	p.m	p.m	p.m	p.m	p.m
WHITWICK departs	9.20	10.20	11.20	1.20	2.15	3.20	5.45	7.0	8.15	10.5
FOREST ROCK app. „	9.25	10.25	11.25	1.25	2.20	3.25	5.50	7.5	8.20	10.10
GREENHILL „	9.30	10.28	11.30	1.28	2.25	3.28	5.53	7.10	8.23	10.15
COPT OAK „	9.35	10.33	11.35	1.33	2.30	3.33	5.58	7.15	8.28	10.20
SHAW LANE „	9.37	10.35	11.37	1.35	2.32	3.35	6.0	7.17	8.30	10.22
MARKFIELD (Green) „		1038		1.38		3.38	6.3		8.33	
MARKFIELD (Q. Head)„	9.40	10.40	11.40	1.40	2.35	3.40	6.5	7.30	8.35	10.25
GROBY „	9.50	10.50	11.50	1.50	2.45	3.50	6.15	7.40	8.45	10.30
LEICESTER (A.S. Rd.) arr.	10.5	11.5	12.5	2.5	3.0	4.5	6.30	7.55	9.0	10.45

BOOK ONE OF BROWN'S BLUE SALOONS FOR YOUR PRIVATE PARTY

Charnwood Publishing Co., Coalville.

Timetable, January 1936 for the Leicester to Whitwick service

STANTON-UNDER-BARDON and LEICESTER

MONDAYS, TUESDAYS, THURSDAYS and FRIDAYS

	W	W	W	S W	W
	a.m.	p.m.	p.m.	p.m.	p.m.
LEICESTER (Stand No. 9) ... dep.	9.25	6.0	6.25	6.35	7.15
GROBY ... ... approx. ,,	9.40	6.15	6.40	6.50	7.30
MARKFIELD (Q. Head) ... ,,	9.50	6.25	6.50	7.0	7.40
CLIFFE HILL ... ... ,,		6.30			7.45
STANTON ... ... arr.		6.35		7.10	7.50

	S W	W		W	W
	a.m.	a.m.	a.m.	a.m.	p.m.
STANTON ... ... dep.	7.5	7.15		8.0	5.0
CLIFFE HILL ... ... ,,		7.20			5.5
MARKFIELD (Q. Head) ... ,,	7.15	7.25			
GROBY ... ... ,,	7.25	7.35			
LEICESTER ... ... arr.	7.40	7.50			

	a.m.	p.m
LEICESTER ... ... dep.	11.5	4.5
GROBY ... ... approx. ,,	11.20	4.2
MARKFIELD (Q. Head) ... ,,	11.30	4.3
CLIFFE HILL ... ... ,,	11.35	4.3
STANTON ... ... arr.	11.40	4.

	S W
	a.m.
STANTON ... ... dep.	7.5
CLIFFE HILL ... ... ,,	
MARKFIELD (Q. Head) ... ,,	7.15
GROBY ... ... ,,	7.25
LEICESTER ... ... arr.	7.40

	a.m.
LEICESTER ... ... dep.	11.5
GROBY ... ... approx. ,,	11.20
MARKFIELD (Q. Head) ... ,,	11.30
CLIFFE HILL ... ... ,,	
STANTON ... ... arr.	

W Workpeople's Services.

	a.m.	p.m.
LEICESTER ... dep.	10.50	3.10
GROBY ... ,,	11.5	3.25
MARKFIELD ,,	11.15	3.35
CLIFFE HILL ,,	11.20	3.40
STANTON ... ,,	11.25	3.45

	a.m.
STANTON ... dep.	10.0
BARDON HILL ,,	10.10
COALVILLE arr.	10.20

	p.m.
STANTON ... dep.	4.0
BARDON HILL ,,	4.10
COALVILLE arr.	4.20

	p.m
STANTON ... dep.	2.50
BARDON HILL ,,	3.0
COALVILLE ... arr.	3.1

Between

LEICESTER (St. Margaret's Bus Station) and WHITWICK (Market Place)

SUNDAYS

	a.m.	a.m.	p.m.	p.m.	p.m.	p.m.	p.m.
LEICESTER (Stand No. 9) dep.	9.20	11.5	2.5	3.40	6.25	8.10	9.50
GROBY ... approx. ,,	9.35	11.20	2.20	3.55	6.40	8.25	10.5
MARKFIELD (Green) ... ,,	9.40	11.25	2.25	4.5	6.50	8.35	10.15
MARKFIELD (Q. Head) ... ,,	9.42	11.27	2.28	4.8	6.53	8.38	10.18
SHAW LANE ... ,,	9.45	11.30	2.31	4.11	6.56	8.41	10.20
COPT OAK ... ,,	9.50	11.35	2.33	4.13	6.58	8.43	10.23
GREEN HILL ... ,,	9.55	11.40	2.38			8.45	10.28
FOREST ROCK ... ,,	10.0	11.45				8.48	10.33
WHITWICK ... approx. arr.						8.53	10.38

L. D. BROWN - MARKFIELD

BROWN'S BLUE BUS SERVICE

PHONE: MARKFIELD 214

TIME TABLE

COMMENCING OCTOBER 1947 AND UNTIL FURTHER NOTICE

WHITWICK			p.m.	p.m.	p.m.	p.m.	p.m.
FOREST ROCK ... approx. ,,	9.20	10.20	1.20	3.20	5.45	7.0	8.15
GREEN HILL ... ,,	9.25	10.25	1.25	3.25	5.50	7.5	8.20
COPT OAK ... ,,	9.30	10.28	1.28	3.28	5.53	7.10	8.23
SHAW LANE ... ,,	9.35	10.33	1.33	3.33	5.58	7.15	8.28
MARKFIELD (Green) ... ,,	9.37	10.35	1.35	3.35	6.0	7.17	8.30
MARKFIELD (Q. Head) ... ,,		10.38	1.38	3.38	6.3		8.33
GROBY ... ,,	9.40	10.40	1.40	3.40	6.5	7.30	8.35
LEICESTER (Stand No. 9) arr.	10.5	11.5	2.5	4.5	6.30	7.40	8.45

TIMETABLES

From the very early days of operation a full and comprehensive timetable was produced. The person responsible for this was the Traffic Manager of the time, Bill Goodman, who looked after the day to day running of services from Markfield (Ashby Road).

With the introduction of the Leicester to Whitwick service, evening and Sunday workings became the norm with all daily services offering a full seven day time table throughout. Market day and some colliery services ran on certain days and at certain times only. The exception to this was during the Second World War and the Suez Crisis when reduced emergency timetables were introduced in line with directives issued by the Traffic Commissioners.

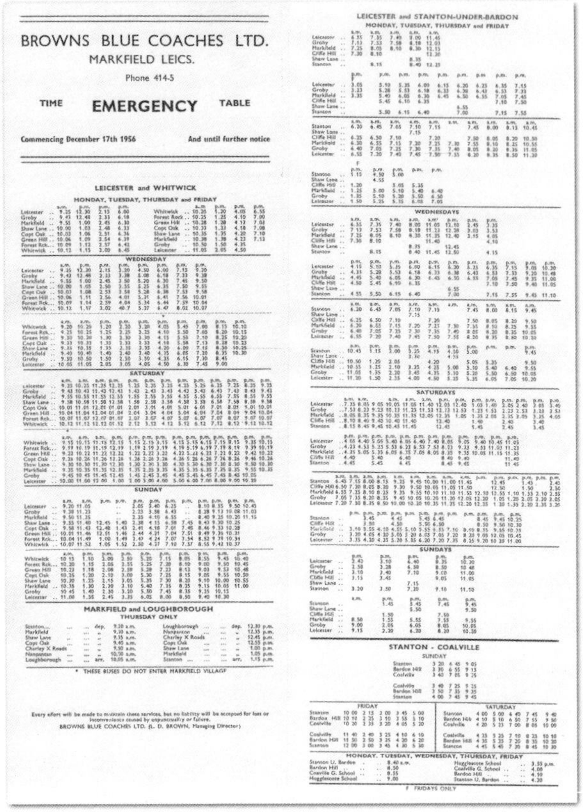
BROWNS BLUE COACHES LTD.
MARKFIELD LEICS.
Phone 414-5

TIME EMERGENCY TABLE

Commencing December 17th 1956 And until further notice

LEICESTER and WHITWICK
MONDAY, TUESDAY, THURSDAY and FRIDAY

LEICESTER and STANTON-UNDER-BARDON
MONDAY, TUESDAY, THURSDAY and FRIDAY

From the start of operations in 1924, through to the mid-fifties, single sheet timetables for the various services were available, a small printed booklet was then introduced which included all services plus some additional timetables featuring the detials of services operated by the constituant companies taken over during the fifties. These were produced in Brown's Blue style and in some cases under the Brown's Blue name, also there were some details regarding Excursions and Tours. These were available at a cost of 3d.

Connecting services were highlighted within the timetable. Passengers were made aware of the possibility of good bus connections at Ashby for Measham, Tamworth, Birmingham, Burton-on-Trent, Melbourne, Derby and Nottingham. Larger printed sheets were placed into wooden timetable cases and positioned at prominent positions en-route, as well as at timing points and all terminal points.

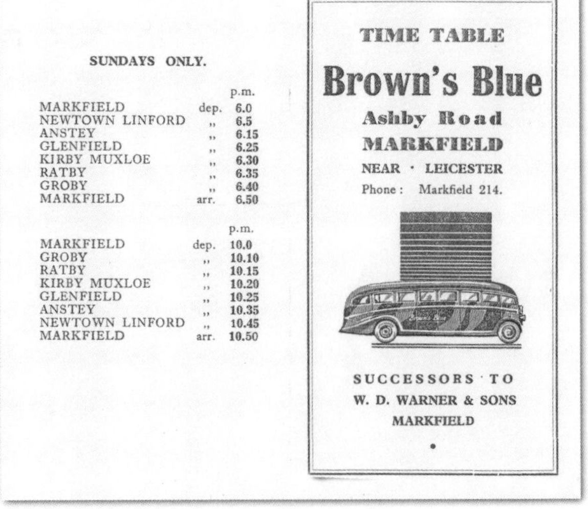
SUNDAYS ONLY.

		p.m.
MARKFIELD	dep.	6.0
NEWTOWN LINFORD	,,	6.5
ANSTEY	,,	6.15
GLENFIELD	,,	6.25
KIRBY MUXLOE	,,	6.30
RATBY	,,	6.35
GROBY	,,	6.40
MARKFIELD	arr.	6.50

		p.m.
MARKFIELD	dep.	10.0
GROBY	,,	10.10
RATBY	,,	10.15
KIRBY MUXLOE	,,	10.20
GLENFIELD	,,	10.25
ANSTEY	,,	10.35
NEWTOWN LINFORD	,,	10.45
MARKFIELD	arr.	10.50

TIME TABLE
Brown's Blue
Ashby Road
MARKFIELD
NEAR · LEICESTER
Phone : Markfield 214.

SUCCESSORS TO
W. D. WARNER & SONS
MARKFIELD

L. D. BROWN : : IBSTOCK

BROWN'S BLUE
BUS SERVICE

TIME TABLE

commencing September, 1950, and until further notice.

S1 IBSTOCK (Hastings Arms) and COALVILLE (Marlborough Square).

Monday, Tuesday, Wednesday & Thursday

	am			W	G						B	pm						B						
IBSTOCK dep.	6 40	7 0	7 15	7 30	8 15	8 35	9 45	......	10 45	11 20	11 45	12 45	1 20	...	2 20	3 50	4 40	4 50	5 18	5 50	5 55	6 40	7 40	8 40
Ellistown ...	6 45	7 5	7 20	7 38	8 20	8 45	9 55	......	10 55	11 30	11 55	12 55	1 30	...	2 30	4 0	4 45	5 0	5 23	5 55	6 0	6 50	7 50	8 50
Hugglescote...	6 50	7 10	7 25	7 43	8 25	8 50	10 0	......	11 0	11 35	12 0	1 0	1 35	...	2 35	4 5	4 50	5 5	5 28	6 0	6 5	6 55	7 55	8 55
COALVILLE.	6 55	7 15	7 30	7 48	8 30	8 55	10 5	......	11 5	11 40	12 5	1 5	1 40	...	2 40	4 10	4 55	5 10	5 33	6 5	6 10	7 0	8 0	9 0

		am				xm					pm												
COALVILLE.	...	7 17	7 35	7 55	8 35	9 5	10 15	10 40	11 15	... ...	12 15	1 15	1 50	2 20	2 50	4 20	...	5 10	5 35	6 10	6 20	7 10	8 10	9 10
Hugglescote...	...	7 22	7 40	7 58	8 40	9 10	10 20	10 45	11 20	... ...	12 20	1 20	1 55	2 25	2 55	4 25	...	5 15	5 40	6 15	6 25	7 15	8 15	9 15
Ellistown ...	...	7 27	7 45	8 3	8 45	9 15	10 25	10 50	11 25	... ...	12 25	1 25	2 0	2 30	3 0	4 30	...	5 20	5 45	6 20	6 30	7 20	8 20	9 20
IBSTOCK arr.	...	7 32	7 50	8x8	8 50	9 20	10 35	11 0	11 35	... ...	12 35	1 35	2 10	2 40	3 5	4 40	...	5 25	5 30	6 30	6 40	7 30	8 30	9 30

Friday

		am			W	G	CB				pm												
Ibstock dep	...	6 40	7 0	7 15	7 30	8 15	8 35	9 20	10 20	11 20	12 20	1 20	...	2 25	3 20	4 20	5 10	5 20	5 55	6 10	6 40	7 35	8 40
Ellistown ...	...	6 45	7 5	7 20	7 38	8 20	8 45	9 30	10 30	11 30	12 30	1 30	...	2 35	3 30	4 30	5 20	5 30	6 5	6 20	6 50	7 45	8 50
Hugglescote	...	6 50	7 10	7 25	7 43	8 25	8 50	9 35	10 35	11 35	12 35	1 35	...	2 40	3 35	4 35	5 25	5 35	6 10	6 25	6 55	7 50	8 55
Coalville arr	...	6 55	7 15	7 30	7 48	8 30	8 55	9 40	10 40	11 40	12 40	1 40	...	2 45	3 40	4 40	5 30	5 40	6 15	6 30	7 0	7 55	9 0

			am								pm				x								
Coalville dep	...	...	7 17	7 35	7 55	*8 35	9 5	9 50	10 50	11 50	12 50	1 50	2 20	2 50	3 45	4 45	5 35	5 45	...	6 35	7 10	8 0	9 10
Hugglescote	...	...	7 22	7 40	7 58	8 40	9 10	9 55	10 55	11 55	12 55	1 55	2 25	2 55	3 50	4 50	5 40	5 50	...	6 40	7 15	8 5	9 15
Ellistown ...	...	...	7 27	7 45	8 3	8 45	9 15	10 0	11 0	12 0	1 0	2 0	2 30	3 0	3 55	[illegible]	5 45	5 55	...	6 45	7 20	8 10	9 20
Ibstock, arr	...	...	7 32	7 50	8x8	8 50	9 20	10 10	11 10	12 10	1x5	2 10	2 40	3 10	4 5	5 [illegible]	5 55	6 5	...	6 55	7 30	8 20	9 30

Saturday

	am			W		CB					pm							B					B							
IBSTOCK dep	6 40	7 0	...	7 30	8 15	8 35	9 20	10 20	11 20	11 40	12 20	12 50	1 20	2 20	2 40	3 15	3 35	4 15	4 35	5 20	5 40	6 20	6 40	7 20	7 40	8 20	8 40	9 20	9 40
Ellistown ...	6 45	7 5	...	7 38	8 20	8 45	9 30	10 30	11 30	11 50	12 30	1 0	1 30	2 30	2 50	3 25	3 45	4 25	4 45	5 30	5 50	6 30	6 50	7 30	7 50	8 30	8 50	9 20	9 50
Hugglescote ..	6 50	7 10	...	7 43	8 25	8 50	9 35	10 35	11 35	11 55	12 35	1 5	1 35	2 35	2 55	3 30	3 50	4 30	4 50	5 35	5 55	6 35	6 55	7 35	7 55	8 35	8 55	9 35	9 55
COALVILLE.	6 55	7 15	...	7 48	8 30	8 55	9 40	10 40	11 40	12 0	12 40	1 10	1 40	2 40	3 0	3 35	3 55	4 35	4 55	5 40	6 0	6 40	7 0	7 40	8 0	8 40	9 0	9 40	10 0

		am									x					x			x		x	x							
COALVILLE.	...	7 17	...	7 55	8 35	...	9 50	10 50	11 50	12 10	12 50	1 20	1 50	2 50	3 10	3 45	4 5	4 45	5 5	5 50	6 10	6 50	7 10	7 50	8 10	8 50	9 10	9 50	10 10
Hugglescote...	...	7 22	...	7 58	8 40	...	9 55	10 55	11 55	12 15	12 55	1 25	1 55	2 55	3 15	3 50	4 10	4 50	5 10	5 55	6 15	6 55	7 15	7 55	8 15	8 55	9 15	9 55	10 15
Ellistown ...	...	7 27	...	8 3	8 45	...	10 0	11 5	12 0	12 20	1 0	1 30	2 0	3 0	3 20	3 55	4 15	5 55	5 15	6 0	6 20	7 0	7 20	8 0	8 20	9 0	9 20	10 0	10 25
IBSTOCK arr.	...	7 32	...	8x8	8 50	...	10 10	11 10	12 10	12 30	1 5	1 40	2 10	3 10	3 30	4 5	4 25	5 5	5 25	6 10	6 30	7 10	7 30	8 10	8 30	9 10	9 30	10 10	10 30

Sunday

		am		pm	B					B		
IBSTOCK dep	...	9 40	10 50	1 40	1 50	2 50	3 50	4 50	5 50	6 50	7 50	9 30
Ellistown ...	...	9 45	11 0	1 45	2 0	3 0	4 0	5 0	6 0	7 0	8 0	9 40
Hugglescote...	...	9 50	11 5	1 50	2 5	3 5	4 5	5 5	6 5	7 5	8 5	9 45
COALVILLE.	...	9 55	11 10	1 55	2 10	3 10	4 10	5 10	6 10	7 10	8 10	9 50

		x					x	x	x			
COALVILLE.	...	11 20	12 10	2 20	3 20	4 20	5 20	6 20	7 20	8 20	9 20	10 0
Hugglescote...	...	11 25	12 15	2 25	3 25	4 25	5 25	6 25	7 25	8 25	9 25	10 5
Ellistown	...	11 30	12 20	2 30	3 30	4 30	5 30	6 30	7 30	8 30	9 30	10 10
IBSTOCK arr.	...	11 35	12 25	2 35	3 40	4 40	5 35	6 40	7 40	8 40	9 40	10 20

B—Connects at Ellistown for Bagworth—Hinckley, etc. x.—Connects with Ashby Service. xm—Connects with Ashby Service Mon. and Weds. only. W—To Memorial Square.
CB—Connects at Ellistown for Coalville and Bagworth. G—Via Grammar School when open.

S2 IBSTOCK (Hastings Arms via High Street) to ASHBY-DE-LA-ZOUCH (Market Street) and SMISBY (Main Street).

Mon., Tues., Weds. & Thurs.

IBSTOCK	...	8 8	9 20	1 5	3 45
HEATHER	...	8 16	9 28	1 11	3 55
NORMANTON	...	8 22	9 34	1 17	4 1
PACKINGTON	...	8 28	9 40	1 23	4 7
ASHBY	...	8 34	9 45	1 28	4 13
SMISBY	...		9 53	SM 1 36	
SMISBY	...		9 55	SM 1 38	
ASHBY arrive			10 3		
ASHBY depart		8 40	10 45	1 45	4 15
PACKINGTON	...	8 46	10 51	1 51	4 21
NORMANTON	...	8 52	10 57	1 57	4 27
HEATHER	...	8 58	11 3	2 3	4 33
IBSTOCK	...	9 8	11 10s	2 10c	4 50ch

FRIDAY

IBSTOCK	8 8	9 20	1 5	4 0
HEATHER	8 16	9 28	1 11	4 8
NORMANTON	8 22	9 34	1 17	4 14
PACKINGTON	8 28	9 40	1 23	4 20
ASHBY	8 34	9 45	1 28	4 26
ASHBY dep	8 40	10 45	1 45	4 35
PACKINGTON	8 46	10 51	1 51	4 41
NORMANTON	8 52	10 57	1 57	4 47
HEATHER	8 58	11 3	2 3	4 53
IBSTOCK	9 8c	11 10c	2 10c	5 c0

Saturday

IBSTOCK	...	8 8	9 20	1 5	4 5	5 33	6 45	7 50	9 35
HEATHER	...	8 16	9 28	1 11	4 11	5 41	6 52	7 58	9 43
NORMANTON	...	8 22	9 34	1 17	4 17	5 47	6 58	8 4	9 49
PACKINGTON	...	8 28	9 40	1 23	4 23	5 53	7 4	8 10	9 55
ASHBY	...	8 34	9 45	1 28	4 28	5 58	7 10	8 15	10 0
SMISBY	...		9 53	1 36	4 38				
SMISBY	...		9 55	1 38	4 40				
ASHBY arrive			10 3						
ASHBY depart		8 40	10 45	1 45	4 50	6 20	7 15	8 40	10 10
PACKINGTON	...	8 46	10 51	1 51	4 56	6 26	7 21	8 46	10 16
NORMANTON	...	8 52	10 57	1 57	5 2	6 33	7 27	8 52	10 21
HEATHER	...	8 58	11 3	2 3	5 8	6 39	7 33	8 58	10 27
IBSTOCK	...	9 8c	11 10	2 10c	5 17c	6 48c	7 45c	9 5	10 35

Sunday

IBSTOCK ...	11 35	5 30	6 48	8 0	9 35
Heather ...	11 41	5 38	6 56	8 7	9 43
Normanton	11 47	5 42	7 2	8 14	9 49
Packington	11 54	5 48	7 8	8 21	9 55
ASHBY ...	12 0	5 55	7 14	8 27	10 0
ASHBY ...	12 5	6 15	7 20	8 45	10 10
Packington	12 11	6 22	7 26	8 52	10 16
Normanton	12 17	6 28	7 32	8 59	10 21
Heather ...	12 23	6 32	7 38	9 5	10 27
IBSTOCK ...	12 30	6 40c	7 45c	9 15	10 35

SM—Smisby: Mon. & Weds. C.—Connects with Coalville Service. ch—Change for Coalville and connect at Ellistown for Hinckley.
Good 'bus connections at Ashby for Measham, Tamworth, Birmingham, Burton-on-Trent, Melbourne, Derby & Nottingham. See Ibstock & Coalville times as the Two connect as indicated.

S3 COALVILLE (Marlborough Sq.) & HINCKLEY (Borough near LLOYD'S BANK) and S6 COALVILLE & BAGWORTH

Mon., Tues., Weds. Thurs.

						x			
COALVILLE dep	6 0	6 55	8 35	...	11 55	2 20	3 0	...	4 55
Hugglescote ...	6 5	7 0	8 40	...	12 0	2 30	3 5	...	5 0
Ellistown ...	6 10	7 5	8 45	...	12 5	2 35	3 10	...	5 5
Bagworth ...	6 20	7 15	8 52	..	12 15	2 40	3 20	...	5 12
Desford Colly. Vill.	...	...	8 57	...	... ...	2 45	...	...	...
Newbold Verdon ...	6 28	7 25	...	...	12 25	...	3 30	...	5 20
Kirkby Mallory ...	6 35	7 32	...	...	12 32	...	3 35	...	5 27
Earl Shilton	6 40	7 40	...	...	12 39	...	3 40	...	5 35
Barwell ...	6 45	7 50	...	...	12 45	...	3 50	...	5 45
HINCKLEY arr	6 55	8 0	...	...	12 55	...	3 55	...	5 55
HINCKLEY dep	7 0	...	8 20	...	1 5	...	4 5		6 0
Barwell ...	7 10	...	8 30	...	1 15	...	4 15	...	6 10
Earl Shilton ...	7 15	8 7	8 37	...	1 22	...	4 22		6 15
Kirkby Mallory ...	7 20	8 15	8 45	...	1 30	...	4 30	...	6 23
Newbold Verdon	7 28	8 25	8 55	...	1 37	...	4 40	x	6 30
Desford Colly. Vill.	...	...	9 0	...	...	...	...	5 5	...
Bagworth ...	7 35	8 35	9 5	10 15	1 50	...	4 50	5 10	6 40
Ellistown ...	7 45	8 45	9 13	10 25	2 0i	...	5 0	5 20	6 48
Hugglescote ...	7 50	8 50	9 18	10 30	2 5	...	5 5	5 28	6 53
COALVILLE arr	7 55	8 55	9 23	10 35	2 10	...	5 10	5 35	6 58

Friday

						x			
COALVILLE dep	6 0	6 55	8 35	11 5	11 55	2 20	3 0	...	4 55
Hugglescote	6 5	7 0	8 40	11 10	12 0	2 30	3 5	...	5 0
Ellistown	6 10	7 5	8 45	11 15	12 5	2 35	3 10	...	5 5
Bagworth	6 20	7 15	8 52	11 25	12 15	2 40	3 20	...	5 12
Desford Colly. Vill.	...	...	8 57	...	...	2 45	...	...	...
Newbold Verdon	6 28	7 25	...	...	12 25	...	3 30	...	5 20
Kirkby Mallory	6 35	7 32	...	...	12 32	...	3 37	...	5 27
Earl Shilton	6 40	7 40	...	...	12 39	...	3 40	..	5 35
Barwell	6 45	7 50	...	...	12 45	...	3 50	...	5 45
HINCKLEY arr	6 55	8 0	...	...	12 55	...	3 55	...	5 55
HINCKLEY dep	7 0	...	8 20	... ...	1 5	...	4 5	...	6 0
Barwell	7 10	...	8 30	... ...	1 15	...	4 15	...	6 10
Earl Shilton	7 15	8 7	8 37	... ...	1 22	...	4 22		6 15
Kirkby Mallory	7 20	8 15	8 45	... ...	1 30	...	4 30		6 23
Newbold Verdon	7 28	8 25	8 55	... ...	1 37	...	4 40	x	6 30
Desford Colly. Vill.	...	...	9 0	... ...	...	...	...	5 5	...
Bagworth	7 35	8 35	9 5	11 35	1 50	...	4 50	5 10	6 40
Ellistown	7 45	8 45	9 13	11 45	2 0i	...	5 0	5 20	6 48
Hugglescote	7 50	8 50	9 18	11 50	2 [illegible]	...	5 5	5 25	[illegible]
COALVILLE arr	7 55	8 55	9 23	11 55	2 1[illegible]	...	5 10	5 30	[illegible]

Saturday

COALVILLE dep	6 0	6 55	8 35	9 25	9 55	12 5	1 55	4 25	6 55	9 25
Hugglescote	6 5	7 0	8 40	9 30	10 0	12 10	2 0	4 30	7 0	9 30
Ellistown	6 10	7 5	8 45	9 35	10 5	12 15	2 5	4 35	7 5	9 35
Bagworth	6 20	7 15	8 53	9 45	10 15	12 25	2 15	4 45	7 15	9 45
Desford Colly. Vill.	...	...	8 57			12 35				
Newbold Verdon	6 28	7 25	...	9 53	10 25	... ...	2 25	4 55	7 25	9 55
Kirkby Mallory	6 35	7 32	...	10 0	10 32	... ...	2 37	5 5	7 35	10 5
Earl Shilton	6 40	7 40	...	10 8	10 40	... ...	2 45	5 15	7 45	10 15
Barwell	6 45	7 50	...	...	10 45	... ...	2 50	5 20	7 50	10 20
HINCKLEY arr	6 55	8 0	...	...	10 55	... ...	3 0	5 30	8 0	10 30
HINCKLEY dep	7 0	...	8 30	...	11 0	... ...	3 10	5 45	8 15	10 45
Barwell	7 10	...	8 40	...	11 8	... ...	3 18	5 55	8 25	10 55
Earl Shilton	7 15	8 7	8 47	...	11 13	... ...	3 23	6 0	8 30	11 0
Kirkby Mallory	7 20	8 15	8 55	...	11 20	... ...	3 30	6 7	8 37	11 7
Newbold Verdon	7 28	8 25	9 7		11 30	... ...	3 40	6 17	8 45	11 17
Desford Colly. Vill.	...	...	...	9 0		12 35				
Bagworth	7 35	8 35	9 17	9 5	11 40	12 40	3 50	6 25	8 55	11 25
Ellistown	7 45	8 45	9 27	9 13	11 50	12 50	3 58s	6 35	9 5	11 35
Hugglescote	7 50	8 50	9 32	T	11 55	12 55	4 3	6 40	9 10	11 40
COALVILLE arr	7 55	8 55	9 37	...	12 0	...T	4 8	6 45	9 15	11 45

Sunday

COALVILLE dep	9 55	1 55	4 25	6 55	9 20
Hugglescote	10 0	2 0	4 30	7 0	9 25
Ellistown	10 5	2 5	4 35	7 5	9 30
Bagworth	10 15	2 15	4 45	7 15	9 40
Newbold Verdon	10 25	2 25	4 55	7 25	9 50
Kirkby Mallory	10 32	2 37	5 5	7 35	9 52
Earl Shilton	10 40	2 45	5 15	7 45	10 4
Barwell	10 45	2 50	5 20	7 50	10 9
HINCKLEY arr	10 55	3 0	5 30	8 0	10 19
HINCKLEY dep	11 0	3 10	5 45	8 15	10 20
Barwell	11 8	3 18	5 55	8 25	10 30
Earl Shilton	11 13	3 23	6 0	8 30	10 35
Kirkby Mallory	11 20	3 30	6 7	8 37	10 41
Newbold Verdon	11 30	3 40	6 17	8 45	10 49
Bagworth	11 40	3 50	6 25	8 55	10 59
Ellistown	11 50	3 58	6 35	9 5	11 9
Hugglescote	11 55	4 3	6 40	9 10	11 14
COALVILLE arr	12 0	4 8	6 45	9 15	11 19

x.—Use Coalville—Ibstock Service and change at Ellistown. T.—Through to Ibstock. i—Change for Ibstock. s.—Change for Ibstock and Ashby.

S4 IBSTOCK—BAGWORTH & DESFORD Colliery Village

	MONDAY TO FRIDAY							SATURDAY			
	am		MT.	F	pm		c	am		c	pm
IBSTOCK ...	...	8 35	9 50	10 20	...	2 20	4 50	...	8 35	9 20	... ...
ELLISTOWN	...	8 45	10 0	10 30	...	2 30	5 0	...	8 45	9 35	... ...
BAGWORTH	...	8 52	10 10	10 40	...	2 40	5 12	...	8 52	9 45	... ...
Desford Coll. Vil. ...		8 57	... ...	... ...	...	...	...	...	8 57	...	... ...
					c						
Desford Coll. Vil. ...		9 0	... ...	... ...	...	...	5 5	...	9 0	...	12 35
BAGWORTH	8 35	9 5	10 15	10 45	1 50	...	5 10	8 35	9 5	...	12 40
ELLISTOWN	8 45	9 13	10 25	10 55	2 0	...	5 20	8 45	9 13	...	12 50
IBSTOCK ...	8 50	9 20	10 35	11 0	2 10	...	5 25	8 50	9 20	...	1 0

MT.—Mon. to Thur. only F.—Fri. only c.—Use Coalville Service and change at Ellistown.

S8 IBSTOCK & DESFORD & intermediate Collieries

MONDAY, TUESDAY, WEDNESDAY, THURSDAY FRIDAY & SATURDAY

	am	*			pm			‡
Ibstock ...	6 5	6 10	6 15	6 20	2 20	...	2 25	9 50
South Coll'y	6 15	6 20	6 25	6 30	2 30	...	2 35	9 55
Ellistown ...	6 20	6 25	6 30		2 35	...	2 40	10 0
Bagworth ...	6 25	6 30			2 40	...		10 5
Desford Coll.	6 30	6 35	...	...	2 45	...	...	10 15
Desford Coll.	6 35	6 40	...	...	2 45	3 0	...	10 15
Bagworth ...	6 43	6 47			2 52	3 7		10 25
Ellistown ...	6 50	6 55	6 30		2 58	3 14	3 0	10 30
South Coll'y	6 55	7 0	6 35	6 40	3 2	3 20	3 5	10 35
Ibstock ...	7 0	7 5	6 40	6 45	3 7	3 25	3 10	10 40

*Sat. 6.10 & 6.15 a.m. as required. Return from Desford 12.15 pm other Coll. as required ‡Also Sun. when ,, Times are approx. A.M. times are from garage circling Ibstock via Melbourne rd and High st. for dep. for various works. P.M. times Hastings Arms.

S7 DONINGTON and IBSTOCK To BARWELL and SHILTON.

WEEK-DAYS
Workgirls' Buses approx. Time Table

	am			am	pm	pm	Sat am
*Donington ...	7 5		Shilton dep	†	6 5		11 5
Ellistown ...	7 10		Barwell	7 50	6 10		11 10
Garage ...	7 15		Nailstone	8 10	6 30		11 30
Ibstock High St	7 20		Ibstock	8 15	6 38		11 38
Nailstone ...	7 30			c	c	c	c
Barwell ...	7 50						
Shilton ...	7 55						

†—Mon. to Fri.
*—Sat. if required
c—Connect to Coalville Service

S5 DONINGTON & COALVILLE

via Crescent Road.

Mon. Tue. Wed. Thur.
Donington: Coalville: 9 25am 7 10pm

FRI
Donington: 4 40 pm
Coalville: 9 28 am 6 15 pm 7 10

SATURDAY
1 40 pm

S9 IBSTOCK to NAILSTONE COLLIERY

Workmen's Service

APPROXIMATE TIME TABLE.

		MONDAYS to SATURDAYS			SUNDAYS
IBSTOCK	dep.	6 10	2 10	9 45	9 45
NAILSTONE	arr.	6 22	2 22	9 57	9 57
NAILSTONE	dep.	6 24	2 42	10 2	10 2
IBSTOCK	arr	6 36	2 54	10 14	10 14

Every effort will be made to maintain these Services, but no liability will be accepted for loss or inconvenience caused by unpunctuality or failure.

September, 1950 L. D. BROWN, Garage: Leicester Road. *'Phone: Ibstock 340.*

J. LAWRENCE & SONS PRINTERS, IBSTOCK

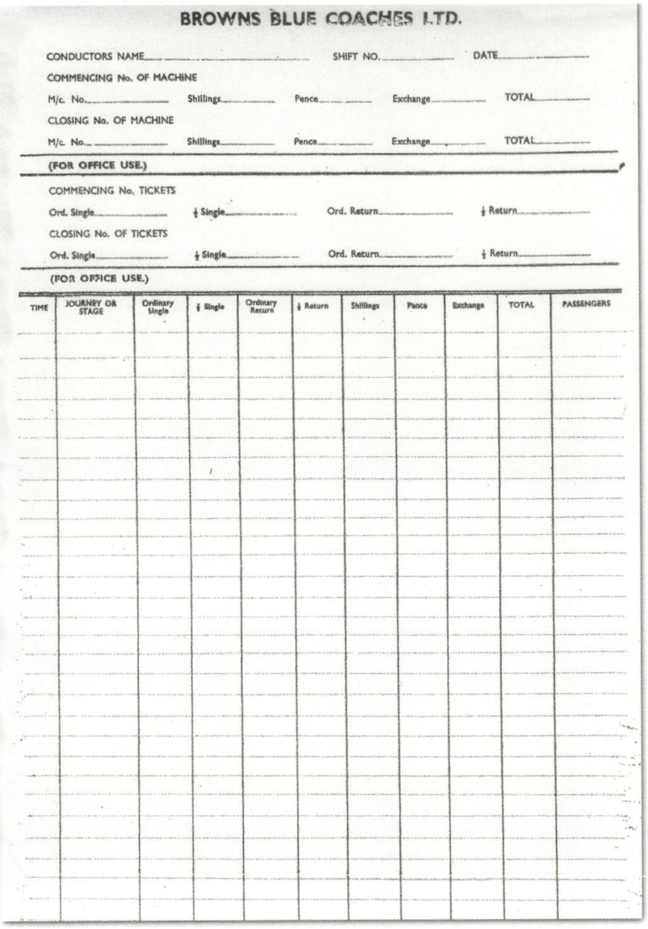
BROWNS BLUE COACHES LTD.

CONDUCTORS NAME ________ SHIFT NO. ________ DATE ________

COMMENCING No. OF MACHINE

M/c. No. ________ Shillings ________ Pence ________ Exchange ________ TOTAL ________

CLOSING No. OF MACHINE

M/c. No. ________ Shillings ________ Pence ________ Exchange ________ TOTAL ________

(FOR OFFICE USE.)

COMMENCING No. TICKETS

Ord. Single ________ ½ Single ________ Ord. Return ________ ½ Return ________

CLOSING No. OF TICKETS

Ord. Single ________ ½ Single ________ Ord. Return ________ ½ Return ________

(FOR OFFICE USE.)

TIME	JOURNEY OR STAGE	Ordinary Single	½ Single	Ordinary Return	½ Return	Shillings	Pence	Exchange	TOTAL	PASSENGERS

PARCELS

In common with many other operators, the carriage of small packages and parcels was undertaken on a predetermined price scale throughout the years of operation. In pre-war days all types of goods were distributed throughout the route network in a less formal manner.

In the more rural areas, farm produce was often left at a pre-arranged point by the roadside ready for collection and delivery. Goods returned would be left in the same manner. These were very tightly knit communities and everybody knew everybody else, the drivers and conductors were well aware of any arrangements which had been made for collection and there was little chance of theft by passers by. If there was nothing to collect the bus would still stop, the driver would give a couple of "toots" on the horn, wait for a wave from the farmer or his wife and if all was well he would carry on.

The Brown family had built up an honourable reputation within the communities it served so well, friendship and trust were without question.

Omnibus Society Collection

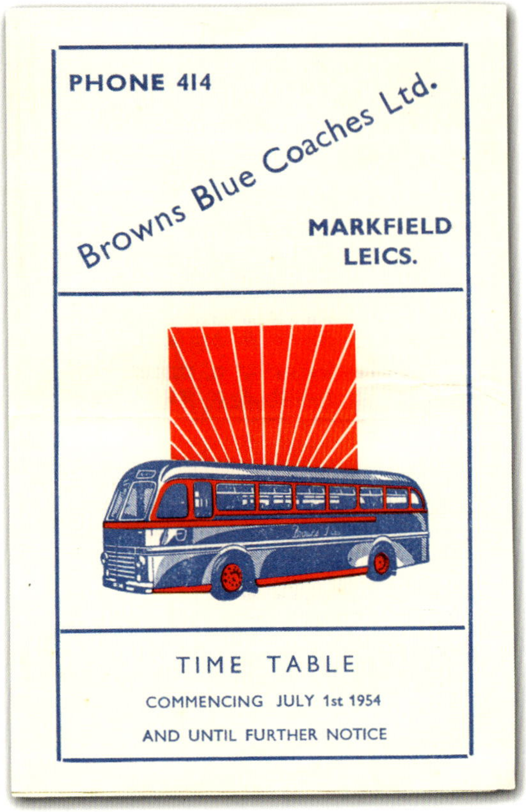

Omnibus Society Collection

Colour Collection Three

For Further Service

It is a testament to the maintenance staff at Browns Blue that with the exception of AEC RT HLW 166, which was very badly damaged in an accident a few months before the sale of the company. All other vehicles in the fleet were sold for further service or private use.

In this colour section we see a few photographs of these vehicles in service with their new owners.

An overcast day in Fraserbrough Scotland, HLX 227 awaits its next departure to Inverallochy; one of four RT's purchased from Browns. **Photo/ Ken Jubb**

HLW 151 is seen here working one of the three "Town Services" operated by Simpsons in Fraserbrough Scotland. **Photo/ Ken Jubb**

Taken at the premises of its new owners Smith, Upper Heyford Oxfordshire in July 1964, HLX 225 is still fitted with Browns Blue destination blinds. **Photo/ Ken Jubb**

Leyland Comet GAY 459 moved into the north east after sale, it is seen here in June 1966 in the yard of Charletons, Newbrough near Hexham. **Photo/ Ken Jubb**

Bury St Edmunds in Suffolk is the location of this excellent view of HLX 89, it is seen here waiting layover time before its return journey to Diss in Norfolk. The very smart livery of Simmonds of Bottesdale completes the picture.
Photo/ Ken Jubb

Although MacDowall's Super Luxury Coaches Ltd of Glasgow, Scotland, operated a large fleet of second hand double deck vehicles for contract work, very few were repainted. In stark contrast to the photograph on the opening page of Colour Collection Two, KWB 82 was still wearing its Browns Blue livery, albeit a little shabby by that time, it stands on waste ground somewhere in Glasgow. The reader with a sharp eye will notice that the rear near side lower deck window is missing. **Photo/ G. Lumb**

Initially passing to MacDowall's Super Luxury Coaches Ltd of Glasgow, Scotland, KWB 85 was subsequently purchased by Patersons of Dalry, Ayrshire, Scotland. It is seen here working the Town Service between Craig Avenue and Blairland in Dalry. **Photo/ Ken Jubb**

The sea forms the backdrop for this fine view of HLW 144 taken in the Simpson depot yard at Rosehearty, Scotland, a change of livery throughout the fleet resulted in larger areas of cream being applied around the windows, which gave the vehicles a much brighter appearance. **Photo/ Ken Jubb**

Taken at the Alexander (Northern) depot only a few yards along the road from Simpsons old premises at Rosehearty, Scotland, HLW 144 was the only RT to pass into the Alexander (Northern) fleet after the takeover on 19th December 1966 it never received Alexanders yellow livery, but it received fleet number NRC 1 and remained in service until withdrawal in 1968. **Photo/ Ken Jubb**

The introduction of the Government Bus Grant scheme in the early seventies brought about the demise of many elderly double deckers in fleets all over the country. Many small independent operators who operated stage carriage services took the opportunity to replace outdated, inefficient vehicles with modern front entrance buses suitable for one man operation. According to whatever mileage percentage was agreed to for stage carriage use, between the operator and the Ministry, a payment would be made towards the cost of replacing older vehicles with new; this would be over a fixed period in some cases for several years. Strict records were kept by the operator and made available to the Ministry to monitor vehicle usage.

Seen here are two of the victims of the rush to modernise fleets, former Gibsons of Barlestone AEC RT HLX145 and AEC Regent 111 KOD 592 (formally Browns) stand in a dealer's yard at Shepshed, Leicestershire, it is doubtful if demand for these vehicles would keep the sales team very busy. **Photo/ Derek Bailey Trevor Follows collection**

CHAPTER IX

UNDER NEW OWNERSHIP

16th March 1963 to 30th June 1968

The face of public transport in north-west Leicestershire had changed forever, gone were the rich deep blue double deckers of Browns Blue to be replaced by sea of bright red vehicles. John Partner (the son of vehicle painter Sid Partner) recalls that they lived in a house overlooking the Markfield garage yard. He remembers that on Friday 15th March the yard was a sea of blue, but by the following Saturday morning it was all red, the transformation had taken place overnight.

Former Midland Red Area Traffic Officer Ken Jubb was responsible for the north-west Leicestershire area. He was involved in the negotiations and recorded the initial vehicle allocation for the Markfield garage. Vehicles were selected from garages throughout the Midland Red network and delivered overnight. They were all made ready for the early morning services. The vehicles involved were as follows:-

MIDLAND RED

S14 SINGLE DECK
4330 from Cradley
4339 from Coalville

D7 DOUBLE DECK
4359 & 4395 from Hartshill
4381 & 4388 from Redditch
4396 from Digbeth
4404 & 4419 from Wigston
4407 from Sandiacre
4418 from Bearwood

D7 DOUBLE DECK (continued)
4438 from Wolverhampton
4474 from Southgate St
4480 from Bromsgrove

In April 1963 a new D9 double decker 5315 was allocated to Markfield, replacing D7 4474 which was returned to Southgate St.

A C3 coach, 4214 was allocated to Markfield from April 1963 to September 1963; this was replaced In October by another C3 4188.

In August 1963 a new D9 double decker 5334 was allocated to Markfield, replacing D7 4381 which was sent to Southgate St.

Finally in November 1963 a new D9 double decker 5357 was delivered to Markfield, replacing D7 4359 which moved to Swadlincote.

Some of the platform staff took advantage of the offer of further employment with Midland Red although office staff and management were not included. Several moved to the main garage at Coalville and some to the Sandiacre and Southgates garage in Leicester. Staff who lived in the immediate Markfield area found it more convenient to stay at Markfield garage until its final closure on 30th June 1968.

Staff would find major differences in the working practices of each company. The informal and more personal atmosphere enjoyed within the smaller family run

This view of Markfield (Shaw Lane) Garage shows Midland Red S17 standing in the A50 entrance/exit. Tucked away in the garage on the right is one of the original Motorway coaches, probably downgraded to normal coaching duties. These three photos were taken at least a year after the takeover. **Photo/ Ken Jubb**

destinations favoured by Midland Red would be an improvement for the travelling public, although the Midland Red "via" displays were not so comprehensive.

This wide angle view of Markfield Garage was taken from the Shaw Lane entrance/exit, it shows various D7s, a D9 standing inside the double deck bay and an S16 to the left. **Photo/ Ken Jubb**

It is interesting to note that the new service from Leicester to Whitwick via the Charnborough Estate was numbered 666. During an interesting conversation with local transport enthusiast John Arnold, he mentioned that the Midland Red had rarely used the same three numbers together anywhere in its very comprehensive route network. I mentioned this to Ken Jubb. He recalls that route number 111 was introduced in the Sutton Coldfield area during the early sixties, certainly before the introduction of route 666. There was however a shortage of route numbers in the 600 series, this being the main allocation for Leicestershire. Many former Browns Blue services received the "C" suffix which was usually allocated to Coalville and its immediate suburbs, but in

MIDLAND RED
ASSOCIATED WITH THE BRITISH ELECTRIC TRACTION CO. LTD. AND BRITISH RAILWAYS
SERVICES
665, 667, 668, 669
LEICESTER
COALVILLE
ASHBY and
BURTON ON TRENT
INCLUDING COMPLETE SERVICE BETWEEN
LEICESTER and BARDON CHAPEL
SERVICE L33
LEICESTER and GROBY (MARTINSHAW LANE)
Completely revised services commencing Saturday, 16th March 1963 and until further notice.
MIDLAND RED
ASSOCIATED WITH THE BRITISH ELECTRIC TRACTION CO. LTD. AND BRITISH RAILWAYS.
Service 670
LEICESTER, STANTON, IBSTOCK, HEATHER and ASHBY
Service 696
LEICESTER, STANTON, IBSTOCK, HEATHER and MEASHAM, SHACKERSTONE or APPLEBY MAGNA
Service C92
COALVILLE and STANTON
NEW AND COMPLETELY REVISED SERVICES COMMENCING SATURDAY, 16th MARCH, 1963 AND UNTIL FURTHER NOTICE.
MIDLAND RED
ASSOCIATED WITH THE BRITISH ELECTRIC TRACTION CO. LTD. AND BRITISH RAILWAYS
Services 666 & 677
LEICESTER
and
WHITWICK
Service 690
MARKFIELD and LOUGHBOROUGH
NEW SERVICES Commencing Saturday, 16th MARCH 1963 and until further notice.
MIDLAND RED
ASSOCIATED WITH THE BRITISH ELECTRIC TRACTION CO. LTD. AND BRITISH RAILWAYS.
Services C76, etc.
COALVILLE, SWANNINGTON and GRIFFYDAM
Services 674, 676
COALVILLE, BELTON, HATHERN and LOUGHBOROUGH
Services 683, 684, 689
COALVILLE, NEWBOLD, WORTHINGTON and MELBOURNE
Complete revision of Service C76, etc. Commencing Saturday, 16th March, 1963 and until further notice.
MIDLAND RED
ASSOCIATED WITH THE BRITISH ELECTRIC TRACTION CO. LTD. AND BRITISH RAILWAYS
SERVICE No. L19
LEICESTER
and
KIRBY MUXLOE
(OAKCROFT AVENUE)
SERVICE No. 664
LEICESTER, KIRBY MUXLOE and BAGWORTH etc.
SERVICE No. 636
LEICESTER, DESFORD COLLIERY and NAILSTONE COLLIERY
Revised Services commencing SATURDAY, 16th MARCH, 1963 and until further notice
MIDLAND RED
ASSOCIATED WITH THE BRITISH ELECTRIC TRACTION CO. LTD. AND BRITISH RAILWAYS
Services 686, 687, 688
COALVILLE
and
HINCKLEY
via
MARKET BOSWORTH
or
NEWBOLD VERDON
Completely revised services commencing SATURDAY, 16th MARCH 1963 and until further notice.
MIDLAND RED
ASSOCIATED WITH THE BRITISH ELECTRIC TRACTION CO. LTD. AND BRITISH RAILWAYS
SERVICES
C87, C97, 687
COALVILLE, IBSTOCK and HEATHER
SERVICES
C80, C86, C89, 688
COALVILLE, BAGWORTH, DESFORD and THORNTON
SERVICE C79
COALVILLE and BATTRAM
Completely revised services commencing Saturday, 16th March, 1963 and until further notice.

the case of the new service between Whitwick and Leicester it was found necessary to use the remaining unused number.This was partly due to the length of the new route 666 and the fact that it and several other similarly numbered routes, served the A50 corridor into Leicester.

Inevitably when major operator and timetable changes take place there are bound to be problems, not all changes suit everybody. The handover went reasonably well, but it was not long before the "honeymoon" period was over. The 22nd March edition of the Coalville Times reported that Ashby Rural District Council had received several complaints concerning the service through Packington and onto Ashby. People in the village expressed concerns that the service before the change was only just adequate, but afterwards the times had changed, causing difficulties with doctors appointments in Ashby. The lunchtime bus had been taken off altogether. The Council agreed to look into the matter.

Residents in Ibstock lobbied their local councillors making a strong protest about the route from Stanton to Markfield because buses were meeting other large vehicles along this section of the route and were forced to reverse in order to pass, resulting in late running. Many passengers were late for work in Leicester. A total of 74 people signed a petition which was handed to the council, who in turn made a protest to the Traffic Commissioners.

In Ellistown, passengers complained that services had been withdrawn from Victoria Road causing difficulties for those wishing to visit the Hospital and passengers in the Newbold Verdon area complained to their local Parish Council about increased fares on the Coalville to Hinckley service, especially the section from Newbold to Barwell, where many local residents used the buses for getting to and from work.The Council made representations to the Midland Red who later said the matter would be looked into.

Alterations in the Measham area mainly involved the cutting back of the Donisthorpe (Cockspur) journeys to terminate in Measham. Midland Red integrated these journeys into route numbers 696 and 670. Route number 712 provided the connection from Donisthorpe to Measham.

RELIANT COACHES

Fate certainly played its part in the post-Browns Blue era for a small group of former employees.They had been part of a football pools syndicate which was fortunate enough to have a considerable win shortly before the closure of Browns Blue.

Ibstock garage foreman Roy Briers, Inspector and tyre fitter George Holmes along with driver Joe Bowley pooled their newly acquired resources to form a new company, Reliant Coaches. They commenced operations on Saturday 16th March 1963, from the former Windridge, Sons and Riley premises, later to be the Browns Blue depot in Melbourne Road, Ibstock. Dennis Gray a former driver with Browns Blue since 1948 was employed to continue his role.They purchased five AEC coaches for use on some of the ex-Brown's Blue contracts and private hires.All vehicles thereafter retained the two-tone light blue livery introduced by Browns Blue on their coach fleet in the late 1950s.

Taken in Memorial Square, Coalville, former Browns Blue AEC Reliance LWH 3 later became the Recovery Vehicle in the Reliant fleet. **Photo/ Keith Wortley**

The vehicles involved were as follows:- AEC Reliance OJU 915, AEC Reliance 4328 UA, AEC Regal III EF 8927, AEC Regal III EF 8928, and AEC Reliance LWH 3 which was later altered to become the breakdown recovery vehicle.

Former Browns employee Jack Neil, who had been Garage Manager at Markfield assisted for a short time with coaching operations before retiring. Jack had been the main stay of Browns coaching activities. He gained valuable experience from working out of the Humberstone Gate Coach Stand and also had a good reputation with his customers in Leicester, ensuring that the work diary in the Browns Blue booking office was always full. This invaluable knowledge helped to steer the fledgling company through its early years.

Seen at the former Browns Blue garage in Melbourne Road, Ibstock, AEC Reliance 4328 UA and AEC Regal III EF 8927 both passed to the newly formed company Reliant Coaches. The garage in Melbourne Road was also included in the sale as well as three other vehicles.
Photo/ John Shilcott Collection

Vehicles manufactured by AEC had featured prominently within the Browns Blue fleet since the early nineteen fifties. Roy Briers was an enthusiastic disciple of AEC products and after the formation of Reliant Coaches was happy to purchase AECs for

AEC Reliance OJU 915 also entered the Reliant fleet; it is seen here inside the Ibstock garage shortly after purchase. Photo/ John Shilcott Collection

many years, new and second hand. The new chassis were purchased and sent to various coachbuilders including Plaxton, Duple and Caetano. After the final AEC Reliance chassis was received registered CUT 402 T and bodied by Plaxton a different direction in vehicle purchasing policy needed to be adopted, The company had purchased several Bedfords, some of which came with the purchase of Deacon and Hardy of Barlestone, new Bedford YRQ and YRT coaches also entered the fleet. Significantly two Volvo coaches also became immediately available at this time, due to a last minute cancelled order by Parks of Hamilton, this would change the face of the Reliant fleet for many years to come.

Roy Briers had enjoyed a close working relationship with one of the sales staff at Moseley Coach Sales at Loughborough. Harry Beardsmore helped with advice and the eventual expansion by the company into continental coach holidays, with the help of the two Volvos and some new Bova's supplied by Moseleys. A contract was drawn up with Riviera Tours to work continental holiday breaks throughout the year.

Local works, colliery and school contracts also played a major part in operations, but by the mid-eighties many collieries had closed. Reliant Coaches worked all the remaining colliery contracts in the area as well as some in Warwickshire until their final demise.

After months of negotiation the management of Reliant Coaches finally agreed to purchase a large area of ground at the old Brickworks in Mill Lane, Heather. Ironically the land was owned by Hubert Bircher who had sold Victory Coaches to Browns Blue back in 1956. Initially garage and office facilities were built with exterior parking for numerous vehicles. Major mechanical repairs and servicing were still carried out at the Melbourne Road premises.

Later extensions to the premises at Heather involved a close association with bodybuilder Caetano and chassis builder DAF. This brought about the construction of new extensive workshop facilities which in turn led to a dealership and service centre being established.

During 1998 Roy Briers decided to "call it a day". He sold Reliant Coaches to Caetano who carried on the business for a further eight years. They had a brief flirtation with the Dennis Javelin chassis, but had started to build up a large fleet of Caetano bodied

DAF coaches, many of which remained in service until the company ceased operation in October 2006, the operators licences terminated in February 2007.

Reliant Coaches had become a well respected operator in its own right in Leicestershire and beyond. The firm foundations inherited from the old company enabled the new management to build upon a strong reputation for good customer care and reliability, which served the area for forty three years.

Gibson of Barlestone purchased the ex-Devon General AEC Regent III KOD 592, which joined sister vehicle KOD 581. It had been suggested but never confirmed, that KOD 592 had received modifications to its

The only double deck vehicle not to be parked at Copt Oak was KOD 592 the former City of Oxford AEC Regent III. It was sold to local operator Gibson of Barlestone and it is seen here shortly afterwards ironically on hire to Midland Red to cover staff shortages.
Photo/ A. A. Turner

front destination aperture as well as being repainted into Gibsons red and cream livery whilst still at Markfield depot. Gibsons also took the opportunity to obtain the entire stock of the eleven Setright Speed ticket machines, some of which passed to other operators via the P.S.V. Ltd. All purchases were loaded into KOD 592 before its short journey to Barlestone.

During April Staplefords of Markfield, who were also based in Shaw Lane, Markfield, purchased AEC Reliance coach VTB 320.

The remainder of the double deck fleet were parked on a car park adjacent to the Memorial Hall at Copt Oak. They were all disposed of at a sale by the Brown Family. There was a strong interest in the vehicles, with all of them seeing further service with other operators from all parts of the country, except for the badly damaged RT which went for scrap. Simpsons of Rosehearty in northern Scotland, tendered for all eight remaining RTs, they successfully acquired four, fortunately for them, the vehicles with the longest COF's (MOT's). Smith of Upper Heyford, Oxfordshire purchased one, as did Simonds of Botesdale and Super of Upminster. Ronsway Coaches of Hemel Hempstead acquired the final RT plus the Roberts bodied Daimler CVD6 and one of the small Bedford C5Z1 coaches. MacDowall of Glasgow obtained three AEC Regents, the two former Sheffield vehicles plus the Weymann bodied AEC Regent which originally came from City of Oxford. Finally the ex-Devon General AEC Regent went to Armstrong of Westerhope in the north-east. Full details of all vehicle sales appear in the Fleet List section in Chapter 12.

Daimler CVD6 FNR 273 was sold to Ronsway, of Hemel Hempstead, these two photos were taken on the premises, the rear view shows FNR out of service, possibly in use as a store, outwardly it appears to still be in good condition.
Photo/ unknown

After the sale several vehicles made their way north of the border, AEC Regents OFC 403 and KWB 85 (below) are seen here with McDowall of Glasgow, still bearing former fleet names, destination blinds and adverts. **Photo/ A J Douglas**

HTT 333 the former Devon General AEC Regent also moved north although not quite so far, Armstrong of Westerhope, near Newcastle purchased this vehicle, it is seen wearing its new livery of pale green and cream. **Photo/ C.W. Routh**

Seen here in service with Smith of Upper Heyford, former RT 408 HLX 225 gives a clue to its recent ownership, it still shows the familiar BB in the upper roof number box. **Photo/ R.H.G. Simpson**

Taken several years after the sale of Browns Blue on 1st April 1977, Bedford SB5 727 AUT is seen here still carrying its original livery with A.R.T. Head, Lutton, Northamptonshire. **Photo/ A.P. Newland**

After withdrawal AEC Regal IV HAY 111 was purchased by Yuill a building contractor from West Hartlepool. Unfortunately frontal damage has occurred. **Photo/ R. F. Mack**

CHAPTER X

THE GARAGES AND THEIR STAFF

Former Engineering Assistant Foreman Ray Morris has kindly compiled this summary of the garage activities and staff based at Markfield Shaw Lane garage. This dates from around the mid-fifties. Apologies to anybody missed.

BROWNS BLUE COACHES LTD

MARKFIELD GARAGE & HEAD OFFICE

Mr L. D. Brown	Managing Director
Mr N. Brown	Chief Engineer
Mr J. Neal	General Manager
Mr A. Hill	Company Secretary
W. Brisley	Engineering Foreman
R. Morris	Engineering Assistant Foreman
C. Bott	Engineer
S. Hull	Driver/Service Engineer
S. Partner	Driver/Painter
G. Brown	Tyre Fitter/ Inspector/Driver
P. Russell	Bodybuilder
J.Arnold	Mechanic
George Rogers	Driver/Mechanic

Mr W. Brisley was in charge of the maintenance department and controlled the stores, he was responsible for ordering spare parts and what he could not buy he made himself. He was a very experienced engineer and would overhaul gearboxes, rear axles, starter motors and dynamos, also turning his hand to more general repairs when required.

Former R.E.M.E engineer Ray Morris was responsible for engine overhauls, fuel injection equipment, electrical repairs, all types of welding and vehicle inspections. He also took his share "behind the wheel" when the occasion arose.

C. Bott was employed on general maintenance duties.

S. Hull serviced the buses and also did some driving.

S. Partner a long time employee was a coach painter/sprayer, although he did a lot of driving.

P. Russell had spent many years working for the renowned bodybuilders Mulliners of Northampton. Percy was a highly skilled craftsmen specialising in body building and upholstery. He converted several half cab coaches to fully fronted vehicles.

The maintenance department was a self contained unit, all of the work required was carried out in house except for crankshaft grinding, crankcase line boring, cylinder head resurfacing and road spring resetting, which were all contracted out to specialists.

General Manager Jack Neil lived in the original house on Ashby Road, Markfield from which Laurie started the business in 1924. The garage adjacent to the house was still used to store a small bus overnight, usually a Bedford OB, this being a precaution against a possible breakdown when the main garage was closed. The refuelling facility at Markfield garage had been totally changed over to diesel oil. The vast majority of the fleet was now diesel powered apart from the few remaining Bedford OBs, the three taxis's and the breakdown vehicle. The petrol pump was still in operation at the house. All petrol powered vehicles were taken there to be refuelled daily. Several former members of staff have had fond recollections about Jack, he was well known for his never ending supply of "Foxes Glacier Mints" and could be relied upon for refreshment whenever the need should arise.

There were three recovery vehicles in use at different times from the end of the war until the takeover. A former military Ford V8 gun tractor fitted with a water bowser body was used to supply the Markfield garage with water. At that time the garage was not connected to the mains. A large winch was fitted for vehicle recovery, however the Ford was unreliable and eventually scrapped. The winch was removed and fitted to the replacement vehicle - an ex-military Bedford QL. The water tank and a metal gantry were also fitted, the latter for use when tree lopping was required. Unfortunately the cab on the QL rotted very quickly due to constant water spillage.

Usually the first drivers back in depot after the morning school runs were given the task of taking the QL down to Jack Neil's house in Markfield where they filled the water tank to replenish the supply at Shaw Lane. The final recovery vehicle was an Austin 4x4 which came from the Government Vehicle Sales Compound at Ruddington. This was a former RAF vehicle and was altered in the company workshops to include a crew cab, extra lighting and a large winch. All three vehicles had been kept at Markfield Garage over the years and recovery work for other operators was carried out when required, establishing a close working relationship with local concerns.

Below is a list of drivers and conductors from the Markfield Depot:

Drivers

John (Jack) White	Lloyd Burton
Eric Partner	Dennis Worth
Harry Knight	Jim Worth
Arthur Maunders	Les Hanagan
Alf Powell	Gerry Prescott
Billy Goodman	Jack Massey
Nat Spencer	George Potter
Dick Clapham	Tommy Liggins
Eddie Donegue	Sid Hull
Ray Vest	Bill Brewin
Jack Clapham	Bill Jones
George Norton	George Hardy
Bill Peet	Eric Simmons
Tom Lambert	George Spence
Joe Weston	Charlie Jolly

Reg's brother Norman spent some considerable time in the R.E.M.E. during the Second World War; an experience he would put to good use when he later took charge of Markfield Garage. He is seen here in 1940 at Biggin Hill in Kent, in charge of a Scammell Tank Transporter.
Photo/ Wynn and Norman Brown

Conductors

Keith Allsopp	George Wardle
Betty Arnold	Hazel Russell
Pauline Brewin	Betty Brown
Enid Brown	Ernie Brindley
Neville Ison	Bert Monk
John Shilcott (usually Ibstock)	

Unfortunately this rear view of one of the Brush bodied Daimlers is a little out of focus. It was taken at Markfield garage yard, immediately to the left is the Canadian Ford V8 Gun Tractor which was modified for use as a recovery vehicle. **Photo/ Wynn and Norman Brown**

The majority of Browns Blue services ran from stand 10 at St. Margaret's Bus Station, Leicester, seen here on the stand is a group of employees they are from left to right – Peter Brewin, Ernie Simmonds, Charlie Jolly, Lloyd Burton, George Wardle, Betty Hill (Burton), Hazel Russell and George Brown (Inspector).
Photo/ Pauline and Lloyd Burton

The lack of destination blinds gives the clue, out of service in Markfield garage yard; Daimler HGC 288 awaits collection by Birds (dealer) staff for its final journey to that ultimate destination, the "cutting torch".
Photo/ Arnold Richardson (Photobus)

Awaiting the same fate, similar vehicle HGC 296 also stands at Markfield garage during September 1959. Repairs and modifications to the bodywork and side windows prolonged the lives of at least two of the Daimlers, but one month after this photo was taken, the last of these vehicles was withdrawn. **Photo/ Unknown**

Also at the Markfield garage yard, Dennis rebuild JU 7854 with Yeates FC37F bodywork is accompanied by ex-LT RT HLX 237 and the breakdown recovery Bedford QL which was also used as a water bowser and tree lopper.
Photo/ R H G Simpson

The three Tilling Stevens vehicles were not the most popular vehicles in the fleet. Initial problems with paintwork followed by further problems with the bodywork soon gave these vehicles a bad reputation. Their saving grace was the fitment of a Gardner engine. They were relatively reliable but they were "plodders" a top speed of 35 m.p.h. made them unsuitable for longer distance coach work.

Norman brown is seen here carrying out some mechanical adjustments to the Gardner engine.
Photo/ Wynn and Norman Brown

Having disgraced itself ex-LT RT HLX 225 has been towed back to the Markfield garage yard for mechanical repairs. Frowned upon by the authorities nowadays the use of a tow chain for recovery was commonplace before the days when vehicle recovery had become a very lucrative business in its own right.
Photo/ John Allen Collection

All types of vehicle maintenance were carried out at Markfield garage, in fact only engine boring; crankshaft grinding and leaf spring tensioning were contracted out. Ex-LT RT HLX 237 awaits its turn to be driven up on the ramp to be steam cleaned, probably for annual inspection. **Photo/ Unknown**

Sadly ex-LT RT HLW 166 was the only vehicle in the Brown fleet not to see further service after the sale; HLW 166 was involved in a serious accident outside the Queens Head public house on the A50 in Markfield during the notorious winter of 1962/63. It is seen here in the Markfield garage yard gradually being stripped of any useful spares, the remains were sold for scrap at the sale. **Photo/ Keith Wortley Collection**

The winter of 1962/63 was the worst since 1947, temperatures well below freezing, plus snow and ice over a long period combined to make this one of the worst winters since records began. Pictured here is (conductress) Pauline Brewin who is carefully making her way across the Markfield depot yard, former Sheffield AEC Regent KWB 85 is seen in the background, on the right is an unknown RT, and on the left is Bedford SB 727 AUT which was only a few months old at this time.
Photo/ Geoff Price Keith Wortley Collection

Pauline Brewin (conductress) and her brother Peter Brewin (driver) with the Harrington bodied Bedford SB which entered service in June 1962. Both Pauline and Peter moved into employment with the Midland Red after the sale.
Photo/ Geoff Price Keith Wortley Collection

BROWNS BLUE COACHES LTD

LEICESTER ROAD IBSTOCK & MELBOURNE ROAD IBSTOCK

Former Ibstock drivers John Shilcott and Joe Bowley have very kindly assisted me with the compilation of this information for the two Ibstock garages, inevitably names will be missed I offer my apologies for this but the passage of time is not kind to even the best of memories.

The two garages at Ibstock were formally owned by companies purchased by Browns Blue. The Leicester Road garage originally belonged to Hipwells, and was taken over in July 1946, and the Melbourne Road garage belonged to Windridge, Sons and Riley Ltd, taken over in August 1956. Maintenance and repairs were carried out at both garages under the watchful eye of Roy Briers. Roy was a very experienced mechanic who knew his vehicles inside out. He was especially fond of AEC products and was proud of the fact that he could change a pre-select gearbox on an AEC RT type between morning and

This pre-war photograph shows Len Briers working for Hipwells. The Dennis Lancet VJ 4672 was sold before the takeover by Brown's Blue, but Len Briers joined Brown's Blue in 1946 working as a driver. Failing eyesight forced him to take on conducting duties in later life.
Photo/ Julie Sanders

afternoon school contracts. Body repairs and painting were usually restricted to Melbourne Road, although some bodywork was carried out by local commercial bodybuilders Bostock and Barsby of Barwell, near Hinckley.

Below is a list of Staff, Drivers and Conductors at the Ibstock Depots:

Mr L. D. Brown	Managing Director
Mr. R. Brown	Chief Engineer
Mr S. Hayes	Office
Mrs B Squires	Secretary
Mr T. Underwood	Manager
Mr. G. Holmes	Inspector & Tyre Fitter
Mr. R. Briers	Garage Foreman
Mr H. Gregory	Mechanic
Mr. C. Thomas	Painter
Mr W. Wade	Upholstery

Drivers

Reg Godfrey	Stan Grucock
Alf Webb	Percy Wright
Aubrey Kinson	Johnny Whitworth
Bill Newmann	Jack Windridge
George Rudin	Joe Bowley
Cliff Ward	John Shilcott
Jim Bown	Jack Baines
Bert Ball	Alf Powell
Harry Holden	Dennis Gray
Gordan Smith	Charlie Clark
Freddie Middleton	Dick Clapham
L. Taylor	George Robinson
Charlie Thompson	Walter Adams
Len Briers	Johnny Cope
William Cope	Joe Wesson
Alvin Stirland	

Conductors

Len Briers	Les Eggington
Bob Ekleston	Joe Jackson
Reg Smith	Jack Massey
Ted Towers	Alf Andrews
Albert Ball	Alec Sperry

The heavily laden BSA Bantam belongs to the R.E.M.E. seated in the middle is Reg Brown. After serving his apprentiship in a local commercial vehicle garage, Reg was conscripted into the army working as a vehicle mechanic, a trade which would prove more than useful in his future career at Ibstock garage. Photo/ Wayne Brown

Circa 1958 Managing Directors

Mrs T. Brown,

Mr R. Brown (Ibstock)

Mr N. Brown (Markfield)

Mr T. Brown / Coachbuilder

Former Warrington (24) Leyland TD1 ED 6463 stands outside the Ibstock garage in Leicester Road. The Dennis alongside is the former Hipwell JU 698, both vehicles were withdrawn from service towards the end of 1949.
Photo/ Omnibus Society Collection

Formally a Devon General AEC Regent with provincial style Weymann bodywork. This vehicle spent all of its life with Browns at Ibstock garage. **Photo/ Peter Yeomans**

Although the main focus of operations at Ibstock garage was stage carriage service, works and school contracts a small amount of private hire work was undertaken. A small fleet of coaches was required, a mixture of AEC Reliance and Bedford SB coaches can be seen here inside the Ibstock garage. **Photos/ Mike Sutcliffe MBE**

Taken inside the double deck garage at Ibstock, from left to right an unknown Bedford SB, the ex-Leicester AEC Regent II DJF 323, a former Sheffield AEC Regent III KWB 85, ex-LT RT HLX 236 and finally former Devon General AEC Regent HTT 333. **Photo/ R F Mack**

Many photographs taken around St. Margaret's Bus Station have one thing in common, George Brown! George was Lawrence Brown's brother. He was based at Markfield Depot, but spent the majority of his time on duty at the bus station looking after the interests of the company. He can be seen here monitoring the loading of the Daimler CD650 which is bound for Heather via Ibstock. **Photo/ Richard Butler**

Chapter XI

The Human Aspect

Although it is interesting to analyse company history, vehicle purchases and withdrawals, routes, depots etc, at the end of the day there is one important element in the equation, human beings! They are basically the only reason we have public transport, whether it is the general public who travel on the buses, or the staff who are employed by the company to make the service work.

I have spent many hours talking to ex-employees, passengers who used the services on a regular basis and former school pupils, who although now in their senior years still remember their journeys to and from the various schools in the area. The following sections contain stories told from memories which have remained for over fifty years, brought to life by a gentle reminder or perhaps a photograph.

Colin Harris formally of Desford Colliery Village and his wife Glynis originally from Bagworth, now living in nearby Thornton have fond memories of travelling to and from Ibstock Secondary Modern School on the twice daily school service from 1960 to the final day on March 15th 1963. All services were double deck operated. They remember one particular driver, Joe Bowley who was regularly rostered for this duty. On the last day they were given some old "Bell Punch" tickets by the conductor as a memento, and they have kept them safe to this day. Other memories include the long light tan coats, similar to warehouse coats, with blue collars with the words "BROWNS BLUE" embroidered on the collars. Staff, especially the conductors always wore them.

Former Garage Hand, Conductor and Driver **John Shilcott** has been very helpful reminiscing about his time spent from the late 1950s through to March 1963. Here are just a few of his memories:

John started his career in the garage workshops helping the coachbuilder. He remembers assisting with the fitting of platform doors to the double deckers and carrying out general body repairs to a variety of vehicles. He was not keen on the painting, the vapour didn't agree with his health and he finally asked for a transfer onto the traffic side of the business.

He was offered a position as conductor which he accepted. He remembers one incident very well. He had started a late Saturday shift on the Coalville to Hinckley service with part-time driver Gordon Smith; they were using the Roberts bodied Daimler FNR 273, and were making their way in service from Ibstock to Coalville. Vehicles starting this route always ran from Ibstock garage in service as buses running "light" did not earn revenue!

As they approached Ellistown Hotel the bus suddenly came to a halt. Unfortunately the driver let out a screech of agony. John ran round to the drivers cab to find Gordon

Seen here in Marlborough Square, Coalville, Daimler CVD6 FNR 273 awaits its next journey to Hinckley. This vehicle gave excellent service throughout its fourteen years with the company, although its temperamental gear change pedal was not for the faint hearted. **Photo/ Richard Butler**

nursing a sore leg, which was trapped behind the gear change pedal and up under the steering wheel. He had fallen victim to the "Devil in the Daimler", Daimler's temperamental gear change pedal, a momentary lapse of concentration and the pedal bit back. Drivers used to the less temperamental ex-LT RT's could be forgiven for this mistake but that did little to alleviate the pain from the sore shin. After a few moments recovering from his misfortune and with the help of John, Gordon was able to reset the pedal and carry on but no doubt the gear changes were dealt with in a more robust manner for the rest of the shift.

When John was old enough he was trained as a driver on the ex-LCT AEC Regent DJF 323. This was the only vehicle in the fleet suitable to obtain a "full" PSV Licence, as it had a manual gearbox, and was used regularly for this purpose. This vehicle also had another special purpose, on the face of it, not a very pleasant one.

The Desford Colliery village service was extended by a couple of miles to Merry Lees Colliery at certain times when a shift change was taking place, Merry Lees was a much smaller mine, so much so that it did not have its own bath and shower facilities. When miners finished their shift they had to make their way round to use the facilities at Desford Pit. Enter the "Dirty Bus" the ex-Leicester Regent which was ideal for this purpose as it still retained its original maroon Rexene seating which could be easily wiped down after the miners, who after emerging straight from the coalface, had travelled for their ablutions.

The "Dirty Bus", AEC Regent DJF 323 was a regular performer on the Desford Colliery service, school contracts and local service duties. It was also used for driver training purposes. John Shilcott passed his test on this vehicle. It spent most of its time with the company allocated to Ibstock garage. Photo/ Peter Yeomans

Towards the end of operations the severe winter of 1962/63 took its toll upon services. I have already mentioned the incident involving the double decker stuck in snowdrifts at Irish Hill, but John tells me that there was a little more to it than that. Upon realising that they would not be able to continue the journey driver Jack Clark and conductor George Wardle decided to gather together their passengers and walk the short distance to the Bulls Head pub at Abbots Oak in order to phone for assistance. It is not known what form of refreshment was offered, but no doubt it was of the warming variety.

Margaret Shilcott remembers "as if it were yesterday" the accident at Ibstock in 1951 involving an ex-Leicester TD3. She was a member of the St John Ambulance Brigade and had been attending the village church parade in Ibstock. They were returning to Coalville along with other members of the group. As the bus approached the sharp bend near the brickworks on the road to Ellistown the driver suddenly noticed a man pushing a pram along the road, he swerved to miss him and the bus struck the grass bank on the opposite side of the road and tipped over. A large bush softened the blow and fortunately injuries were only minor. Most passengers were able to continue their journey, however the bus suffered major damage and was withdrawn and scrapped shortly afterwards.

Although running transport can be a serious business there are times when certain incidents may seem in retrospect, a little amusing. Several vehicles were being used for contract services which started early in the mornings from Leicester. Several drivers lived

The Foden was one of several vehicles parked overnight at St. Margaret's Bus Station, for the convenience of drivers living in Leicester who needed to make an early start for works contracts. Problems with vagrants and theft forced the management to alter these arrangements. Secure parking was arranged at a number of locations within the city.
Photo/ Roy Marshall

in Leicester and were able to take on their various duties from the bus station. The Foden was one of the vehicles used regularly for these duties. On the night 19th December 1953 a vehicle belonging to Brown's Blue, thought to be the Foden was found by a police officer parked on a grass verge adjacent to Pindar Road on the main A50 near the Leicester City boundary. On further examination he found a man on board who at first denied taking the bus from St. Margaret's Bus Station. It was thought that this person was taken to Leicester by a group of men, after a night out in Coalville for a prank. He was dropped at the bus station and after ringing the police they ran off.

On 23rd January 1954 a policeman was patrolling the bays at St. Margaret's Bus Station when he heard someone trying to start an unattended bus belonging to Brown's Blue. Upon further investigation he found what turned out to be the same person sitting in the drivers cab with his hands on the steering wheel. After questioning, the person admitted that he was going to take the bus back to Ibstock and leave it outside the garage. He was subsequently charged with both offences at Leicester Magistrates' Court, he was found guilty of both offences, disqualified from driving for five years and also fined £16.00. Mr A. H. Headley who was representing the accused said that unfortunately the guilty party was of simple mind.

I had the pleasure of visiting former conductress **Betty Hill**, who now lives in a nursing home in Coalville. In her long working career she has turned her hands to almost any job ranging from shovelling coal into sacks

Public Houses were a natural timing point for bus services, Drivers and conductors struck up a good working relationship with landlords and various small businesses en-route, toilet facilities and the provision of boiling water for refreshments were always welcome.

Former LT RT HLW 160 awaits its next journey to Leicester from The Crown Inn at Stanton-under-Bardon, the driver can be seen in his cab, the "Clippie" is probably sorting the Billie Can. Photo/ Ken Jubb

to factory work, but she says the job that she enjoyed the most was her sixteen years working as a bus conductress.

She joined Browns Blue as a young woman in 1948 working through to the final day in March 1963. She then transferred to the Midland Red and carried on for another year. She tended to work a regular shift which generally started with the 06.20 a.m. Stanton-under-Bardon to Leicester service. The downside of this shift was when worked on a Saturday it involved very long hours starting at the garage at Markfield at 06.00 a.m. and not finishing until 11.45 p.m. There were however two reasonable breaks, but long hours nevertheless.

Bus crews and their affection for a cup of tea have often been the butt of many jokes. Betty says that Browns Blue platform staff were no different. She always worked from Markfield depot, the routes working out of Leicester to Whitwick, Ibstock, Measham and many points in between were dotted with timing points, usually at bus stops adjacent to public houses. She recalls that arrangements were made with the publicans to refill "Billie" cans which were exchanged by the conductors as the bus waited at the timing point.

Betty recalls the camaraderie and banter shared with the staff of all of the other operators even though, when on the road they were competing. Her second husband Joseph (Henry) Hill served on the Midland Red for over twenty five years, Betty still has the company certificate to prove it.

Social events such as Christmas parties were originally held at the Cooperative function rooms in High Street, Leicester, later events were moved to the Fox and Goose public house at Coalville.

The date of this group photograph is uncertain; however it is thought to be circa 1959, the Brown family appear in the centre lower front surrounded by members of staff, wives, and friends mainly from Markfield garage.
Photo/ Audrey and Ray Morris

It was not uncommon for Markfield crews to exchange shifts with Ibstock crews on Saturdays, Betty remembers this well, she says it was nice to have a change of scenery sometimes. She found football and speedway specials a little tedious; she had little interest in going with the drivers to watch the sport and preferred to stay with the buses sweeping and cleaning out the interiors.

One annual social event which Betty fondly remembers was the company Christmas dinner and dance, held at the Leicestershire Co-operative Societies function room in the basement of their large store in High Street, Leicester and later at the Fox and Goose public house in Coalville. Betty was proud to be a part of Browns Blue's operations and was very sad when the company closed down.

Driver **Joe Bowley** worked for Browns Blue for ten years before joining four fellow employees as part of the management team at new venture, Reliant Coaches. Joe remembers one Saturday morning, again driving Daimler FNR 273, he had just left Newbold Heath bound for Coalville when as he approached a sharp left hand bend the accelerator spring let go. Apparently with the Daimler engine the opposite effect to that expected would occur, instead of losing all of its revs the bus accelerated into the bend causing the conductor to be thrown off balance, Joe managed with difficulty to bring the vehicle to a halt. One of the skills required of a driver in those days was ingenuity. Joe removed his braces, tied one end round the cab roof mounted sun visor, wrapped the middle part around the throttle pedal and tying the other end off under the cab floor, he continued the journey to Coalville without any further problems, apart from maintaining his dignity keeping his trousers up!

Lloyd and Pauline Burton (Brewin) were both employed at Markfield depot. Lloyd was only 21 years old at the time, and he served for just over a year with the company until the takeover. He remembers the camaraderie and good times he had with his colleagues. He says that drivers usually drove their own vehicles but when doing overtime or covering for other staff, a variety of vehicles and duties were worked. Lloyd's bus was ex-LT RT HLW 144. He remembers the final evening, as the buses entered the garage after service the double deckers were taken to a parking area adjacent to the pub at Copt Oak, parked in two rows awaiting sale. Lloyd and Pauline both transferred along with several other members of staff to the Midland Red, staying at the Markfield depot

Pauline served as a conductress from about 1956 until the end. She fondly remembers fellow conductress Hazel Russell who had originally worked for Warners at Markfield before moving to Brown's Blue at the time of the takeover. One particular lady she will never forget lived in a cottage at Copt Oak. Her name was Mrs Siddens, and she was a regular user of the Leicester to Whitwick service. She often gave the driver and conductor a small bag containing a couple of

Although working for Browns Blue for only a relatively short period Lloyd Burton remembers the final days of operation well. He drove former LT RT HLW 144 for most of the time. He married Conductress Pauline Brewin and both moved onto employment with the Midland Red after the sale. Happily retired they still live in Markfield. Photo/ R F Mack

cigarettes and a bar of chocolate. She kept chickens and would often send fresh eggs on the bus down to Markfield. The Thursdays only - Stanton – Markfield – Nanpantan – Loughborough service was usually worked by a Bedford 29 seater and an arrangement was made to stop outside the first farm, in Stanton Lane, on the right hand side where two elderly ladies would pass over a wicker basket and two shillings. Mrs Siddens would board the bus at Copt Oak and conduct the vehicle to and from its destination, calling at Charley

Platform doors would certainly be a welcome addition to the various double deck vehicles operated by the company, especially during the harsh winter of 1962/63.

Hazell Russell and her driver Peter Brewin await their next part duty in Markfield Depot yard.
Photo/ Geoff Price Keith Wortley Collection

The smaller 29 seat Bedford OB coach was the mainstay of the more rural routes, such as the Ibstock to Ashby service, the Stanton to either Loughborough or Anstey routes and the Stanton to Coalville service. Duplication of the main routes was also undertaken during busy peak time hours. Formally Rudins Bedford OB ENR 294 with Duple bodywork is seen leaving Markfield depot by the A50 exit **Photo/ A P Newland Collection**

Cross Roads to pick up a group of farmers wives before carrying on to Nanpantan Cross Roads which was the last pickup point. Trent Motor Traction ran buses from there on as this was part of another protective agreement.

Upon arrival in Loughborough the bus would be parked near the old swimming pool, next to the park. It would be left unlocked so that passengers could return with their shopping, leaving it on the bus. The driver would take the basket which was full of butter to a shop in Swan Street, where it was weighed and exchanged for cash. The departure time was midday, returning and dropping off en-route. Mrs Siddens departed at Copt Oak and the basket was left at the farm, after sounding the horn to alert the two ladies. Browns Blue not only provided a bus service, but a community lifeline which was much appreciated by local residents in the area.

Pauline lived in Stanton-under-Bardon at the time. She recalls early mornings, standing waiting near her home for the bus to pick her up at start of duty; sometimes the Commer two stroke would be used. She remembers the distinctive sound that could be heard pulling out of Markfield garage onto Stanton Lane nearly two miles away. Paulines brother Peter also worked at Markfield as a driver and she fondly remembers a fellow conductress Hazel Russell who worked for Warner's at Markfield and after the takeover carried on working for Browns Blue for many years.

Pauline Brewin is seen inside the top deck of one of the Weymann bodied double deckers.
Photo/ Geoff Price Keith Wortley Collection

Old friends **Terry Riley and Bob Pearson** who both live in Stanton-under-Bardon remember Browns Blue buses very well. Terry and his father both drove for Parsons before the takeover with Terry driving the Bedford and his father the Leyland Lion, neither of which entered Brown's Blue service.

Bob Pearson worked in Leicester, travelling on Brown's service twice daily, six days a week. He remembers purchasing a book of tickets on a Monday morning for seven shillings (old money), about thirty five new pence, using one ticket per journey. He handed a ticket to the conductor who in turn clipped it and handed it back.

John Partner son of **Sid Partner** who worked for Laurie Brown for all of his life remembers some good times at the garage. During 1959 when the livery change on the coaches was being considered, Sid painted Johns push bike in the new colours as an experiment. He says it must have been successful because shortly afterwards one of the coaches appeared freshly painted in the new livery. Periodically Sid would disappear with a tin of paint and his paint brush for a couple of days. He could be found along the service routes painting the bus stop flags which were of the old cast iron type.

Taken on a "dead mileage" journey to Blackpool Eric Partner often broke the journey by calling at his wife's mothers house in Sale, Cheshire. His mother in law is seen with Eric's son Raymond standing next to Dennis Lancet III FUT 527. Photo/ Brian Partner

Sid also drove, as did John's brother Eric, both enjoyed private work, but worked stage carriage services when the need arose. The proprietors of a company Frank and Bill Loweth of Torpedo Wools in Leicester always asked for Sid to take them to a Hunt Ball each year in one of the taxis. They became much the worse for wear as the night wore on and on the return it was Sid's job to see them into home, and if necessary put them in bed, needless to say he was well rewarded financially for his efforts.

Obviously taken from a newspaper cutting, this picture shows Sid Partner wearing his flat cap and overauls. Sid carried out most of the painting at Markfield. He was a very capable craftsman with both spray and brush painting. Sid was also an experienced coach driver and was just as happy behind the wheel.
Photo/ Leicester Mercury

Eric Partners son Brian recalls that his father drove the Dennis Lancet FUT 527 for much of the time. Blackpool holiday service duties

Taken on a day excursion to Trentham Gardens, Stoke-on-Trent. Members of the Markfield Chapel line up for the camera. The minister can be seen on the top right and driver Sid Partner is a little lower to the right. The Leyland Comet was used on the occasion. Photo/ Brian Partner

usually had an element of "light" running within their operating schedule. Brian remembers the family travelling on such occasions as far as Sale in Chesire, they would be dropped of at his grandmothers to stay for a few days and picked up on an empty return journey later.

Having fun in the coach park at Skegness are driver Nat Spencer (top left), Eric Partner (top middle), Brian Partner (lower left), Ray Partner (2nd left), Carol Jones (centre), just in the background is Margaret Partner, Mrs Jones (centre right) and holding the mop, driver Charlie Jolly. Photo/ Brian Partner.

Wayne Brown son of Reg Brown says there were many occasions when Browns Blue were involved in regular community activities on a pre-arranged daily basis. As a young teenager he remembers when they lived near to the garage in Leicester Road he would travel on a bus, usually a Bedford OB coach, but sometimes a double decker which would be used to collect pre-cooked school dinners in large insulated aluminium containers from the central kitchen at Ibstock High School, and transport them to the Junior school in Melbourne Road and onto Battram school three miles away. These were heavy awkward containers, usually quite warm which the driver had to handle himself. This was easy enough on the large platform area of a double decker, but a very different kettle of fish (excuse the pun) on the steps of a Bedford OB. This duty was affectionately known as the "Naffi Run".

Walter Higgins of Great Glen, Leicestershire wrote an article in the Leicester Mercury several years ago recalling his memories of his youth in Markfield village. He remembered the "named" buses which were operating in the area "The Nippon" was operated by a Mr Bill Bown and was renowned for its unreliability, although it had a fair turn of speed. Walter also recalls the first vehicle operated by Lawrence Brown, a Chevrolet truck which could be easily converted into a small bus with wooden slatted seats known as the "Nancy". This was of course the first vehicle purchased by Lawrence Brown in late 1923.

Walter remembers when his father was in charge of the football team at the village school they used the bus to transport them to away matches, but the most memorable occasion took place on 25th September 1925 when he and his pals travelled in a very cramped bus to see Leicester City play Arsenal at Filbert Street Football Ground, unfortunately Leicester lost the game 0-1.

Former Leicester City Transport driver **Michael Sleath** recalls his school days spent firstly in Kirby Muxloe and later at Anstey Martin High School. Michael says that after he left the infants school in Kirby he, along with numerous other children were transferred to Anstey Martins which meant a bus journey of about five miles. The buses used were a mixture of Browns Blue double deckers and a couple of coaches with RTs being the norm although the two Daimlers FAY or EJU occasionally appeared. He remembers the ex-Victory AEC coach number HAY 111 noticing at the time that although a fully fronted saloon, it had a separate cab within the body. He also recalls that when moving up into the second year he still caught the Browns Blue buses, but thereafter all first year students travelled on Astill and Jordan vehicles.

Mr Roland Bagnall remembers his childhood days spent in the Coalville area. Regular visits to the market on Fridays were usually followed by a ride home to Hugglescote on their local bus service run by a Mr Ball. After the war Roland got married and rented a small cottage at Copt Oak, next door to Mrs Siddens who I mentioned previously. Roland would cycle from Copt Oak towards Whitwick every morning at about eight o'clock. He was regularly passed by one of Brown's double deckers running "light" to start its journey from Whitwick to Leicester. As I have said before, this was the most exposed section of any bus route in Leicestershire and when the weather was bad the bus would stop to enable Roland to place his bicycle on the rear platform and resume his journey, all unofficial of course but a good example of the community spirit offered by Brown's Blue and its staff.

Ted and Mary Pepper now live near Markfield. They both have fond memories of wartime travel on Brown's Blue. One particular incident which comes to mind was on the morning after the Coventry Blitz on 14th November 1940, and in the period until 19th November 1940 when Leicester and its suburbs were suffering heavy bomb damage.

Mary's parents were concerned about the safety of their children and decided to put the children on the Brown's Blue bus which left St. Margaret's Bus Station at 9.00am. The drivers and conductors knew the family well and would put the children off at the appropriate point, bearing in mind it was difficult to communicate in those days. Having the same concerns, Mary's grandmother who lived in a cottage next to the Bulls Head public house at Greenhill jumped on the first available bus from Whitwick to Leicester in order to go and collect the children. Needless to say both buses passed in opposite directions reversing the situation, but it was all sorted out in the end!

Ted lived on a farm a few yards along the road from Mary's grandmother. They all knew each other very well and he would often meet them off of the bus. In later years romance blossomed and Ted remembered his courting days. On Saturday nights they would catch the bus into Whitwick to go to the pictures. Unfortunately the last bus left Whitwick (Market Place) at 10.00pm, but the film usually finished at about 10.10pm. Needless to say Ted and Mary have missed the end of numerous films.

While on the subject of wartime memories, **Bernard Hipwell** who is related to the Hipwell family (former bus proprietors) at Ibstock. He remembers his journeys from Woodhouse Eaves to the South Charnwood School near Thornton. Brown's often used the Bedford on this run. Bernard says that they were never the most comfortable vehicles to travel on. He also remembers Brown's buses coming to the village to pick up the ATS girls and to transport prisoners of war to their various work places.

Over the years Brown's Blue operated school services to many parts of Leicestershire, **Malcolm Skerritt** from Leicester recalls school journeys to Lutterworth Grammar School which is at the opposite end of the county, to Brown's base. Malcolm also says that Broomfield Hall Sunday School in Leicester always used Brown's buses for their Sunday Summer outings.

Former driver **George Potter** worked at Markfield in the mid-fifties. He says that there was normally a shortage of double deck drivers for service work, which was often supplemented by coach drivers. These drivers would be trained up for double deck licences as soon as possible. He remembers three or four vehicles being parked up in St. Margaret's Bus Station overnight in order to work the early morning Powerjets (English Electric) contract to Whetstone and the Clutsom Kemp factory contract to Coalville. However the bays in the bus station were not the most secure places to leave vehicles unattended and arrangements were altered after a short time, which seems to confirm recollections by **Michael Clark** who now lives in Norfolk. He recalls about three coaches being parked up in a secure yard at the rear of the Emmanuel Church in New Park Street, Leicester.

Local historian **Alan Briggs** from Hinckley recalls bus services in the Hinckley, Barwell and Earl Shilton areas. His memories go back to around 1950 when Brown's were operating the former Coalville (Marlborough Square) to Hinckley service taken over from Hipwells in 1946. The service terminated at The Borough until 1960, after which a new bus station was opened in Waterloo Road.

He says that coaches were used initially alongside the Roberts bodied Daimler FNR

Taken in the newly opened bus station at Hinckley, former LT RT HLX 89 awaits its return journey to Coalville. The destination blind would benefit from some attention to the tensioner. **Photo/ Ken Jubb**

273, until the introduction of the former LT Daimlers during 1953. The buses were well used especially during the peak time hours with workers from the numerous factories commuting from the outlying villages. Market days were also very busy. He remembers travelling on Brown's to Scout camp at Kirby Mallory and occasional journeys to Earl Shilton and Coalville. The last bus on a Saturday night was always busy, leaving The Borough in Hinckley at 11.00pm, about the same time as the Midland Red route 658 to Leicester, which ran parallel with Brown's service as far as the turn to Kirby Mallory at the bottom of "Shilton Hill" on the A47, where they parted company. Brown's service turned left and made its way through to Coalville via Newbold Verdon, with the Midland Red carrying straight on via Desford Cross Roads and onto Leicester. The Midland Red double decker always carried a full standing load, but there was usually some space available on Brown's.

Assistant garage foreman at Markfield **Ray Morris** and his wife **Audrey** have very vivid memories of an unusual holiday. The story goes that a party had booked a coach for a two week holiday in the south of France. Shortly before the departure date four members of the group cancelled with two places being taken virtually straight away, Ray and his wife decided to book the remaining two. Ray was travelling as an onboard mechanic, although he did more than his fair share of the driving. Upon arrival, imagine their surprise when they found that the main

Audrey and Ray Morris enjoyed many trips out on the coaches; they are seen here standing in front of one of the Bedford SBs KAY 674 with locally built Yeates bodywork. Photo/ Audrey and Ray Morris

group were in fact Naturists and their holiday was to be spent in a Nudist Colony! I will resist the obvious puns about bodywork.

John (Jack) White was employed as a coach driver. It is a complete mystery why John acquired the nickname "Jack". He was never known by that name before his nine years at Brown's Blue and never since, but was always called Jack by his colleagues. He drove one of the Dennis vehicles with a half cab. In fact he was given DRF 530 on his first morning. He remembers very well the few weeks prior to the Coronation in 1953. He drove down to London on a daily basis to carry out tours of the Coronation procession route. Bearing in mind there were no motorways in those days it must have been a very long tiring day, but as John says these were jubilant times in a period when people were looking for some light relief from the post war austerity period.

Upon the arrival of the two twenty nine seat Bedfords in 1958, one was allocated to Ibstock, the other went to Markfield. PUT 660 was given to John as his regular vehicle. To supplement his income, John along with several other coach drivers would turn his hand to conducting on service in the evenings and during the winter months when private hire and tour work were at a minimum, John would conduct full time.

When the RTs arrived he remembers spending some evenings scraping off paper adverts and rubbing down in preparation for repainting. He enjoyed his nine years at Browns but the need for greater financial rewards plus more regular hours would inevitably force him to return to his original job in a local shoe machinery factory.

John (Jack) White used Dennis Lancet DRF 530 for many years before receiving this Bedford C5Z1 PUT 660 with Duple bodywork, it is seen here on service duties in St. Margaret's Bus Station on a wet day during May 1958, a month after entering service. Photo/ Roy Marshall

We have visited **Wynn and Norman Brown** on several occasions spending many hours chatting about their memories of Brown's Blue history.

It was not unusual to all see members of the Brown family helping out with the day to day running of the company. Wynn and Norman lived in the house at the top of the entrance

Happy days, Norman Brown enjoys a few moments with the young members of the Saffron Lane Working Mens Club.
Photo/ Leicester Mercury

onto Stanton Lane. Wynn remembers the many times when she was called upon to perform conducting duties. She also recalls many hours spent working around the garage performing office duties, cleaning and vehicle preparation.

They still remember the terrible winter of 1962/63 mentioned earlier. The Bulls Head at Abbots Oak near to Greenhill, between Copt Oak and Whitwick was a popular public house attracting customers from the local area, many travelled by Brown Blue. On one particular day blizzard conditions had virtually cut of the area with snow drifts many feet high burying much of the landscape, a narrow roadway was cut through the snow enabling the bus service to resume, much to the relief of the pub regulars who soon made their way to the hostelry only to find that the entrance doors were buried in snow. Undaunted by the problem the driver manoeuvred the double decker bus close to the building so that patrons could climb out of the open side windows and into the bedroom windows of the pub. I can only imagine the antics on the return journey after a few pints had been consumed.

Norman enjoyed his days out on the coaches, as can be seen from the photograph. He valued his relationship with the customers and was keen to give his passengers a good day out. Norman talks about the many times when he worked the Leicester to Great Yarmouth excursions. Never very popular with local coach drivers as travelling east on the old A47 the early morning sun could be a problem. Wardley Hill near Uppingham, Rutland was to say the least a challenge to all, but the most experienced drivers and crossing the busy A1 at Wansford could only be described as a nightmare. He says something of a respite came in the form of a refreshment break at the Coronation Café, halfway between Thorney and Guyhirn Bridge. This was a very popular stop for coaches, the drivers were always welcomed and after signing "the book" would be offered a free cooked breakfast. They all sat together in their own reserved area. It must be said that these breakfasts were not good for the waistline.

Suitably refreshed the driver could look forward to heavy traffic queues at Kings Lynn, Swaffam and the notorious Norwich ring road, before entering Great Yarmouth via the Acle Straight.

This was a long and tortuous journey for the driver usually taking about five and a half hours each way, thus making time spent in Great Yarmouth relatively short. Upon loading for the return journey, there was usually a strong smell of boxed kippers in the air, these were quickly dispatched to the rear luggage compartment. The journey would be non-stop until it was time for the customary pub call usually taken at a variety of public houses in either Wansford, Tixover or Uppingham. This often depended on which of the numerous coaches had reached there first, a good old sing song would round off the day.

Norman admits that these were very long days, upon returning to the garage the coach was refuelled, swept and mopped making the coach ready for the next days work. It goes without saying there was no tachograph.

After the sale of the company, Wynn and Norman joined with younger brother Terry and moved into the garage trade. They occupied premises opposite Stanton Lane, Markfield and later Wynn and Norman purchased a small garage business in Anstey. They emigrated to Australia for a few years before returning to this country in 1970. Several years were spent in the licensed trade before retiring. Wynn and Norman now live in Kettering, Northamptonshire.

Finally I would like to say it has been a great pleasure to talk to so many people both within the Leicestershire area and also further afield. I have been impressed by their enthusiasm and determination to assist me in recording this important part of local history for future generations to study and enjoy.

MICK GAMBLE

Colour Collection Four

UPDATING IN 2012

Much has changed in North West Leicestershire during the past fifty years; the area has been dissected by the M1 Motorway and to a lesser extent by the A42(M), enabling developers to construct a large warehouse and distribution development such as the Bardon Business Park which has the benefit of easy motorway links.

This has helped to offset the numerous redundancies brought about by the full scale Coalfield closures during the seventies, only one opencast site remains operational, it is situated at Ravenstone to the west of Coalville.

In complete contrast the local quarries have expanded their operations supplying all

Ashby road, Markfield where Lawrence Brown started his business on January 1st 1924 these were the premises he worked from. To this day the large sloping roof to the right of the house remains, this was originally part of the garage in which he stored his buses, this remained in use throughout the life of the company. The house was occupied by Markfield Garage Manager Jack Neil in later years. **Photo/ The Author**

All Saints Road, Leicester during the nineteen twenties most operators used a variety of public house yards in central Leicester as a terminal point, later a somewhat improvised bus station was sited underneath the Great Central Station in All Saints Road. The area was quite busy in those days with numerous factories, shops and the busy railway station all close by, unfortunately time has taken its toll, most of the factories have closed, the shops have been demolished and the railway ran its final services in 1969.

All Saints Road is now a very run down area of Leicester in need of urgent refurbishment which is long overdue.
Photo/ The Author

types of Road Stone, Ballast and Tarmac Products to all parts of the country on a twenty four hour timescale.

The local landscape was devastated by abandoned pit heads, mine workings and the subsequent subsidence. As part of a fresh look at the environment and the wider "Green" issues the government declared the area from Ratby near Leicester to Swadlincote in South Derbyshire as a regeneration area to be known as the National Forest.

There are now many leisure facilities throughout the area such as the Ashby Canal Museum at Moira, Snibstone Discovery Park, Coalville and last but not least "Conkers" a Nature Reserve and Discovery Centre devoted to the future of the National Forest.

What about the local transport connections? Many of the former Browns Blue services still exist albeit in much modified form, some are operated by Arriva (Midlands) who closed their main garage in Coalville in 2010, a small number of buses are kept at an outstation in Hugglescote but the remainder of the output is handled by the main depot at Thurmaston near Leicester. Other services are operated by smaller local companies often subsidised by the County Council, however due to the present financial situation these services are under constant review.

Shaw Lane Garage opened during 1936 Shaw Lane Garage was the main base for operations until the company's sale in 1963. Much of the mechanical engineering work was carried out at this depot. The garage is still used as a transport depot by a haulage contractor and much of the original buildings remain intact (top), however for safety reasons the exit onto the A511 (former A50) has now been closed (bottom). **Photo/ The Author**

Leicester Road, Ibstock was for many years the premises of a local Building Contractor, this has now been transformed into a residential area, however the houses opposite still remain the same. **Photo/ The Author**

Melbourne Road, Ibstock has remained in use as a bus depot since Browns Blue sold out to the Midland Red in 1963, Reliant Coaches used it for several years after which local bus company Country Hopper took over the site, they still operate from this garage. **Photo/ The Author**

Hinckley Bus Station never the most inviting of places has changed little during the past fifty years. Service revisions, cuts, vandalism and a constant lack of funding has reduced the bus station to a single roadway, the rest of the original loading area has been altered into car parking. Elderly bus shelters and boarded up toilets complete a very dismal picture. **Photo/ The Author**

Marlborough Square, Coalville still serves as a bus terminal point for the Hinckley and Ibstock local services but most of the surrounding buildings have taken on new identities. The two cinemas are now a Bingo Hall and a Soft Furnishings outlet and the Trustees Savings Bank is now a Pub/Restaurant. **Photo/ The Author**

Duncan Road, Leicester was the former premises of J. H. Hill – a small coach business taken over on 1st January 1952. It was only a small yard capable of holding two or three coaches; it was used as an outstation by Browns Blue to accommodate vehicles working local contracts and private hire duties. It has now been redeveloped into a home for the elderly. **Photo/ The Author**

St. Margaret's Bus Station, Leicester was totally rebuilt in 1985 replacing the old concrete shelters with a modern glass fronted structure where the buses load and unload in herringbone fashion, a prominent feature seen in numerous photographs taken in the old bus station is the former Leicester Printers Ltd building which still survives, albeit now boarded up. **Photo/ The Author**

Browns Blue Garages was a company formed by Norman Brown and his younger brother Terry after the sale of the bus company. The premises are still on the opposite side of the road to the original bus garage, one hundred yards past the Flying Horse roundabout towards Coalville. The subsequent owners have retained the name which is a poignant reminder of a company with a memorable past. **Photo/ The Author**

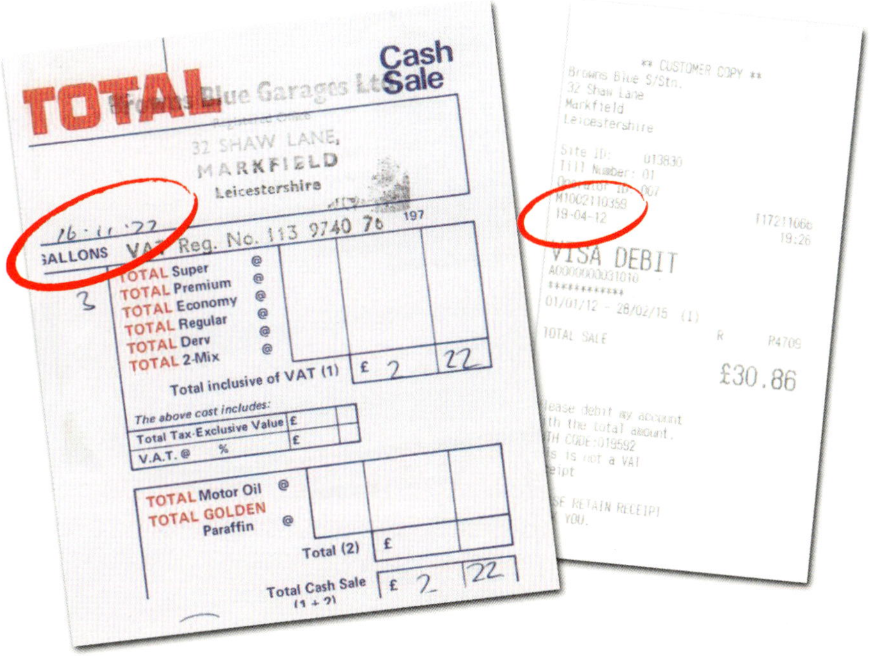

Almost thirty five years separate the written receipt dated 16th November 1977 (left) from the computer generated receipt dated 19th April 2012 (right), major changes have also taken place to the method of payment, cash has almost been replaced by plastic bank cards but the most noticeable difference is the price of fuel. After the sale by Norman and Terry Brown many years ago, several subsequent owners have chosen to keep the well established company name.

Chapter XII

Fleet Lists

I could not have produced this fleet list without taking the opportunity to acknowledge the P.S.V. Circle, the late Paul LeFevre, Allan T Condie and also Geoff Price, Keith Wortley and Paul Blanchard who have all spent many hours compiling these lists without which, it would have been impossible for me to include such a full and comprehensive record of vehicle movements.

Some abbreviations which will help you to understand the following details

GMC General Motors Corporation
TMS Tilling Stevens Motors
L.T. London Transport
LCT Leicester City Transport
NCB Northern Coachbuilders Bodywork
PMT Potteries Motor Traction

L.D.Brown and Brown's Blue Bus Service
1st January 1924 to 1st July 1954

Reg No	Chassis & No	Body type	Date New	Date Acquired	Withdrawn
NR 3581	Chevrolet 26223	B14 Dixie type	1/23	c1923	12/25 scrap
NR 5701	Chevrolet 41159	B14	1/25	1/25	3/27 to Watson Coalville
NR 7669	Chevrolet R 6485	B??	11/25	11/25	7/28 to E Stanton, Great Bridge
NR 8172	Chevrolet X 8092	B14	3/26	3/26	5/27 to Horton, Lutterworth
UT 521	Dennis 30 CWT 51598	B18	3/27	3/27	6/32 to lorry
UT 2055	Chevrolet LM 18338	B14	2/28	2/28	4/29
UT 3563	Chevrolet LO 42811	B14	8/28	8/28	9/32
UL 2658	Renault R1 362525	B20	4/29	4/29	c5/31 burnt out
UT 5687	Chevrolet LQ 55202	B14	7/29	7/29	11/31 burnt out

Reg No	Chassis & No	Body type	Date New	Date Acquired	Withdrawn
UT 6608	GMC T42 422858	B20	3/30	3/30	c/38
UT 8193	Maudsley MLB3C 4940	B32 Willowbrook	1/31	1/31	12/41 to Fieldsend Salford
UT 8355	Commer Invader 6TK 28165	B20 Willowbrook	1/31	1/31	5/36 to Archer Attleborough
UT 9568	Bedford WLB 108024	B20	10/31	10/31	5/35 to Worsdell Earith
UT 3163	GMC T30E 303426	B26	5/28	c/32 ex-Peberdy Enderby	2/35 to Matthews Shouldham
JU 2562	Bedford WLB 109144	B20F Willowbrook	7/33	7/33	9/44 to Barker Mablethorpe
JU 4723	Dennis Lancet 170713	C32F Willowbrook	8/34	8/34	10/45 to Applewhite Dunham
JU 6301	Bedford WTL 874785	C25F Willowbrook	6/35	6/35	2/45 to Thomas North Muskham
ARW 864	Bedford WTL 873466	C25F	3/35	c/1936 ex-Bunty Coventry	unknown
JU 9148	AEC Regal 6622017	C32R Burlingham	7/36	7/36	3/41 to War Dept & Kent War Agric. Committee
AJU 230	Bedford WTB 112319	C26F Duple	6/38	6/38	2/51 unknown
AJU 358	AEC Regal 6622182	C35F Mulliner	6/37	6/37	c12/39 to War Dept not traced
BAY 18	Bedford WTB 112319	C26F Duple	6/38	6/38	1/51 unknown
ANR 216	Dennis Lancet 2	DP39F Willowbrook	9/37	3/39 ex-Toone Billesdon	9/54 to Daisy Broughton
BJU 779	Bedford WTB 8942	C26F Willowbrook	3/3	c/40 ex-Philips Enderby	12/45 to King Worthing

Reg No	Chassis & No	Body type	Date New	Date Acquired	Withdrawn
HRF 102	AEC Regal 6622984	C32F Harrington Rebodied, Yeates FC39F 5/52	5/39	3/40 ex-Hemmings Pensnett	with W.D. 7/40>2/47 and returned 9/60 unknown
BDB385	AEC Regal 6622372	C32F Burlingham	7/39	c/40 ex-Edwards Marple	12/57 to Fry Ellesmere Port
VD 6508	AEC Regal 6621927	FC32F Pickering	c/36	c/40 ex-Jackson Guisborough	6/48 to Wesley Stoke Goldington
CNR 224	Bedford OWB 10160	B32F Roe	10/42	10/42	9/47 to Shaw, Oldham
CNR 436	Bedford OWB 12336	B32F Roe	2/43	2/43	8/49 to Morton Potter Leicester
CUT 344	Bedford OWB 19603	B32F Duple	4/44	4/44	7/48 to East Glam Nelson
CUT 345	Bedford OWB 19505	B32F Duple	4/44	4/44	3/50 to Showman
BNR 59	Leyland TS8 300202	C37F Plaxton Rebodied c/49 Burlingham C33F	4/39	c/46 ex W.D. orig. Windridge	11/58 unknown
UT 5848	Reo Pullman GEA73	B20F Bracebridge	9/29	6/46 ex Hipwell 5 Ibstock	12/46 to Hawkins Loughborough
UT 6207	Reo Pullman GEA61	B20F Bracebridge	11/29	6/46 ex Hipwell 2 Ibstock	7/46 to Hawkins Loughborough
JU 698	Dennis Lancet 170102	DP32F Willowbrook	6/32	6/46 ex Hipwell 7 Ibstock	9/49
JU 3054	Dennis Lancet 170433	C32F Willowbrook Rebodied c/51 Harrington ex FV 1550	11/33	6/46 ex Hipwell 4 Ibstock	3/55 to Daisy Broughton

Brown's Blue operated a total of eight Bedford OWB buses, five were purchased new and three were bought second hand, two from Lloyds of Nuneaton and one from Hipwell of Ibstock. The third vehicle delivered new was CUT 344 It was withdrawn after only four years service and sold to East Glam Motors, Nelson 8/48, to Knoill, Cross Gates 10-49 (as photo), mobile shop 6/58. It was subsequently re-bodied by an unknown coachbuilder to a style not dissimilar to that of a Duple "Vista" design with larger window apertures. **Photo/ R. H. G. Simpson**

The last vehicles to be delivered before the reorganisation to a limited company on 1st January 1954 were two Bedford 'S' type coaches with Yeates Riviera bodywork. KAY 674 is seen here in Ibstock. **Photo/ Ken Jubb**

Reg No	Chassis & No	Body type	Date New	Date Acquired	Withdrawn
JU 7225	Dennis Lancet 171005	DP38F Willowbrook	10/35 ex Hipwell 3 Ibstock	6/46	9/57 to scrap
RC 1525	Dennis Lancet 170419	DP35F Willowbrook	8/33	6/46 ex Hipwell 8 Ibstock	c/53 unknown
AAY 6	Dennis Lancet 2 175137	DP39F Willowbrook Rebodied 4/55 Yeates FC37F	12/36	6/46 ex Hipwell 6 Ibstock	9/59 Body to EAY 58
AAY 679	Bedford WTB 111077	C26F Duple	3/37	6/46 ex Hipwell 10 Ibstock	4/52 to Ward Oakham
AUT 287	Bedford WTB 112073	C26F Duple	3/38	6/46 ex Hipwell 9 Ibstock	1/51 mobile shop
CUT 343	Bedford OWB 19582	B32F Duple	4/44	6/46 ex Hipwell 11 Ibstock	3/50 Mountain Transport London SW3
DAY 146	Bedford OWB 30130	B32F Duple To B28F	9/45	6/46 ex Hipwell 12	8/56 to Bagworth Colliery
AUE 27	Dennis Lancet 2 175004	DP39F Willowbrook	4/36	c/46 ex Edwards Bishops Itchington	5/54 to N.C.B. Newcastle
DWD 795	Bedford OWB 12206	UB32F Mulliner to UB28F c/46	1/43	c10/46 ex Lloyd Nuneaton	c/47 unknown
DWD 796	Bedford OWB 12203	UB32F Mulliner to UB28F	1/43	c10/46 ex Lloyd Nuneaton	c/47 to Millbrook Plymouth
ED 6463	Leyland TD1 72087	H30/26R Massey	5/31	4/46 ex Warrington 24	12/49 to scrap
ED 6464	Leyland TD1 72088	H30/26R Massey	6/31	12/46 ex Warrington 25	12/49 to scrap
ED 6560	Leyland TD1 72136	H30/26R Brush	8/31	1/47 ex Warrington 37	3/50 to scrap
DUT 554	AEC Regal 06624797	C35F Duple	3/47	3/47	10/59 to scrap
EAY 58	Dennis Lancet III 164J3	C35F Yeates Rebodied 10/59 Yeates FC37F from AAY 6	5/47	5/47	3/63 to Forsell Leicester

Reg No	Chassis & No	Body type	Date New	Date Acquired	Withdrawn
EJU 260	Dennis Lancet 3 297J3	C35F Yeates Rebodied 2/60 Yeates FC37F from JU 7854	10/47	10/47	2/62 to Forsell Leicester
EJU 541	Daimler CVD6 15230	H30/26R Brush rear door c/52	1/48	1/48	9/60 to scrap
EJU 786	Bedford OB 64283	C29F Yeates	2/48	2/48	4/58 to scrap
WW 6814	Leyland TS2 60028	C30F Shearing	8/28	12/47 ex Warner Markfield	c/48 to Hawkins Loughborough
FV 1550	Leyland TS2 61276	C32F Harrington	1/31	12/47 ex Warner Markfield	3/51 accident Body to JU 3054
TH 7165	Maudsley SF40 5319	DP36F Burlingham	4/36	12/47 ex Warner Markfield	c/48 to Gibson Barlestone
JU 7854	Dennis Lancet 2 175002	DP39F Willowbrook Rebodied 4/55 Yeates FC37F	1/36	12/47 ex Warner Markfield	12/59 Body to EJU 260
DRF 530	Dennis Lancet 2 175066	DP39F Willowbrook	7/36	12/47 ex Warner Markfield	9/54 to Daisy Broughton
AUT 694	Bedford WTB 112157	C26F Willowbrook	5/38	12/47 ex Warner Markfield	c/49 to Howlett Quorn
GLL 939	Leyland LT8 302511	C35F Duple	c/39	12/47 ex Warner Markfield originally BHS 268 to Hayley & Weller Draycott	c/54
CNR 362	Bedford OWB 11429	B32F Mulliner	12/42	12/47 ex Warner Markfield	12/49 to MacMullen Birmingham
CNR 480	Bedford OWB 12531	B32F Roe	3/43	12/47 ex Warner Markfield	2/50 to Miller Cirencester
ENR 792 FLT 9	TSM K6LA7 9292	C32F Theale to C33F later	6/48	6/48	3/58 to Rose Bolton

Reg No	Chassis & No	Body type	Date New	Date Acquired	Withdrawn
EUT 52 FLT 8	TSM K6LA7 9295	C32F Theale to C33F?	7/48	7/48	11/57 to Valley Supplies Bacup
EUT 947 FLT 14	TSM K6LA7 9309	C32F Theale to C33F?	1/49	1/49	11/57 to Hughes Gomersall
FAY 517	Daimler CVD6	H30/26R Brush rear doors c/52	1/49	1/49	11/61 to scrap
FJU 533	Foden PVSC6 27752	FC33F Burlingham	6/49	6/49	1/58
FNR 273	Daimler CVD6 15331	H30/26R Roberts rear doors c/52	9/49	9/49	3/63 to Ronsway Hemel Heampstead
JF 5873 FLT 1	Leyland TD3 4623	H26/24R Metro-Cammell	5/34	9/49 ex Leicester 270	12/53 to scrap
JF 5875 FLT 3	Leyland TD3 4626	H26/24R Metro-Cammell	5/34	9/49 ex Leicester 272	12/53 to scrap
JF 5878 FLT 4	Leyland TD3 4628	H26/24R Metro-Cammell	5/34	9/49 ex Leicester 275	12/53 to scrap
JF 5883	Leyland TD3 4632	H26/24R Metro-Cammell	6/34	9/49 ex Leicester 280	7/51 accident to scrap
FUT 452	Dennis Lancet III 700J3	C35F Duple	3/50	3/50	9/60 to Todd Whitchurch
FUT 527 FLT 11	Dennis Lancet III 707J3	C35F Duple	3/50	3/50	10/62 unknown
GAY 459	Leyland CPO1 493972	C33F Burlingham	5/50	5/50	3/63 to Mid-Tyne Acomb
JF 5008 FLT 2	Leyland TD3 3421	H26/24R Metro-Cammell	12/33	6/50 ex Leicester 266	6/55 to Showman
HAY 601	Dennis Lancet 2 175807	DP39F Willowbrook	10/36	5/51 ex W.D. (orig. Rose) Holbeach JL3733	4/54 to Gravelling Corby
GUT 398 FLT 42	Leyland PSU1/11 510028	C41F Duple	6/51	6/51	3/63 to Taylor Tamworth
GUT 399 FLT 43	AEC Regal IV 9821E462	C41C Yeates	9/51	9/51	9/60 to Williams & Davies Southsea

Reg No	Chassis & No	Body type	Date New	Date Acquired	Withdrawn
GUT 400 FLT44	AEC Regal IV 9821E545	C41C Yeates	8/51	8/51	9/60 to Plaistow Wheatley
DRY 777	Bedford OWB 19576	C29F Duple 7/49	4/44	4/52 ex Hill	11/59 to Mobile Shop
HBC 634	Bedford SB 1639	C33F	1/51	4/52 ex Hill	3/63 to Richards Spraxton
HGC 288	Daimler CWA6 12526	H30/26RD Duple	c/46	4/53 ex L.T. D161	8/58 to scrap
HGC 292	Daimler CWA6 12543	H30/26RD Duple	3/46	4/53 ex L.T. D165	10/59 to scrap
HGC 296	Daimler CWA6 12544	H30/26RD Duple	c/46	4/53 ex L.T. D169	6/58 to scrap
HGF 806	Daimler CWA6 12595	H30/26RD Duple	c/46	4/53 ex L.T. D179	2/59 to scrap
FUT 777	Dennis Lancet III 759J3	C35F Yeates	2/50	8/53 ex Parsons Stanton	2/59 to Lorry
EWM 372	Daimler CWA6 12230	H30/26RD Duple	9/45	12/53 ex Southport 62	7/58 to scrap
GLX 905	Daimler CWA6 11832	H30/26RD Duple	c/44	12/53 ex L.T. D 19	6/58 to scrap
GYE 64	Daimler CWA6 12043	H30/26RD Duple	c/45	12/53 ex L.T. D74	10/58 to scrap
JNR 926	Bedford SB 18592	C37F Yeates	9/53	9/53	2/62 accident to scrap
KAY 674	Bedford SBG 25575	C38F Yeates	5/54	5/54	3/63 to Don Bishops Stortford
KAY 675	Bedford SBG 26184	C38F Yeates	5/54	5/54	3/63 to County Brentwood

Taken in Marlborough Square, Coalville former Sheffield AEC Regent III KWB 82 awaits its next journey to Hinckley. The 'S' type Midland Red single decker at the rear is also bound for Hinckley, albeit by a different route via Market Bosworth. **Photo/ Ken Jubb**

Although the Daimler CD650 KHP 998 is interesting enough in itself, the most unusual part of this photograph is the vehicle behind. The two Brush bodied Daimlers were always associated with Markfield garage, Daimler CVD6 FAY 517 appears to be operating a journey to Ibstock, normally the preserve for Ibstock based vehicles. Both vehicles are seen in Marlborough Square, Coalville. **Photo/ Julie Sanders Collection**

BROWNS BLUE COACHES LTD
1ST JULY1954 TO 15TH MARCH 1963

Reg No	Chassis & No	Body type	Date New	Date Acquired	Withdrawn
VJ 6068	Dennis Lancet 170459	C32F Yeates (1949 body)	3/34	7/54 ex Rudin Ibstock	12/57 to scrap
AJU 879	Bedford WTB 111619	C26F Duple	7/37	7/54 ex Rudin Ibstock	8/54 to Desford Colliery Sports Club
BNR 631	Bedford WTB 19931	C26F Duple	7/39	7/5 ex Rudin Ibstock	11/54 to Mobile Shop
AMS 257	Bedford OWB 23750	B28F SMT	1/45	7/54 ex Rudin Ibstock	-/54 to Mobile Shop
ENR 294	Bedford OB 72926	C29F Duple	2/48	7/54 ex Rudin Ibstock	9/61 to Mobile Shop
HJU 434	Bedford SB 7145	C33F Duple	1/52	7/54 ex Rudin Ibstock	3/63 to York Chorlton
NJU 948	Commer Avenger 3 T85A0446	C41F Duple	6/56	6/56	3/63 to Cathedral Gloucester
KHP 998	Daimler CD650 16925	H31/25RD Roe	1/51	12/56 ex Beckett Bucknell	12/60 to scrap
GKL 765	Leyland TD7 305818	H28/26RD Weymann	7/40	11/56 ex Maidstone & District DH7	7/58 to scrap Bird (dealer)
OJU 915	AEC Reliance MU3RV1600	C43F Duple	5/57	5/57	3/63 to Reliant Ibstock
ONR 771	AEC Reliance MU3RV1601	C43F Duple	6/57	6/57	3/63 to Bland Cottesmore
KUG 3	Leyland PS1/1 461094	FC33F Duple	3/47	12/57 ex Wallace Arnold	11/62 to Hanagan Leicester
KUG 6	Leyland PS1/1 462361	FC33F Wilkes & Meade	3/47	12/57 ex Wallace Arnold	9/60 to Morris Wigan
KUM 521	Leyland PS1/1 472852	FC33F Wilkes & Meade	7/47	12/57 ex Wallace Arnold	3/63 to Morris Wigan

Reg No	Chassis & No	Body type	Date New	Date Acquired	Withdrawn
LNW 990	Leyland PS1/1 472047	FC33F Burlingham	3/48	12/57 ex Wallace Arnold	3/63 unknown
EAY 180	Leyland PS1/1 462853	C35F Yeates (1950 body)	5/47	1/58 ex Windridge Ibstock	9/60 to Morris Wigan
KAL 99	AEC Regal III 9621E323	C33F Burlingham	10/48	1/58 ex Windridge Ibstock	9/60 to Coppock, Sale (dealer)
FUT 339	Bedford OB 125514	C29F Duple	1/50	1/58 ex Windridge Ibstock	10/62 to Williams Leicester
HAY 111	AEC Regal IV 9821E511	C41C Gurney Nutting	7/51	1/58 ex Windridge Ibstock	3/63 to Yuille W. Hartlepool
PUT 659	Bedford C5Z1 2374	C29F Duple	3/58	3/58	3/63 to Ronsway Hemel Hempstead
PUT 660	Bedford C5Z1 2381	C29F Duple	5/58	5/58	3/63 to Hornsby Ashby
HLX 227	AEC Regent III 0961157	H30/26RD Weymann	8/47	8/58 Ex-L.T. RT410	3/63 to Simpson Rosehearty
HLX 237	AEC Regent III 0961054	H30/26RD Weymann	9/47	7/58 Ex-L.T. RT420	3/63 to Super Upminster
HLW 166	AEC Regent III 0961174	H30/26RD Park Royal	9/47	8/58 ex L.T. RT179	3/63 accident to scrap
HLX 225	AEC Regent III 0961171	H30/26RD Weymann	7/47	9/58 ex L.T. RT408	3/63 to Smith Upper Heyford
HLW 151	AEC Regent III 0961040	H30/26RD Park Royal	8/47	9/58 ex L.T. RT164	3/63 to Simpson Rosehearty
HLW 144	AEC Regent III 0961152	H30/26RD Park Royal	7/47	10/58 ex L.T. RT157	to Simpson Rosehearty
HLW 160	AEC Regent III 0961154	H30/26RD Park Royal	9/47	10/58 ex L.T. RT173	3/63 to Ronsway Hemel Hempstead
HLX 236	AEC Regent III 0961042	H30/26RD Weymann	9/47	10/58 ex L.T. RT419	3/63 to Simpson Rosehearty
HLX 89	AEC Regent III 0961300	H30/26RD Park Royal	1/48	12/58 ex L.T. RT272	3/63 to Simonds Botesdale

Albert Richard Hipwell

Leicester Road Garage, Ibstock.t/a Green Bus Service
Acquired 6/46 Services to Coalville, Leicester and Coalville to Hinckley
The garage became Brown's base in Ibstock

Reg No	Chassis & No	Body type	Date New	Date Acquired	Withdrawn
UT 1357	Reo Sprinter 14630	B20F Willowbrook	7/27	7/27	1/31 scrap
UE 4670	Reo Pullman W3326	B20F Willowbrook (new body) 1933	7/27	c11/33 ex Johnson, Bedworth	12/35
UT 1930	Chevrolet LM 17893	B14F Willowbrook	11/27	11/27	1/30 Lindsey C. Council
UT 5848	Reo Pullman GEA73	B26F Bracebridge	8/29	8/29	6/46 to Brown
UT 4280	Reo Pullman GE42	B26	9/29	9/29	11/33 to Dawson Wisbeach
UT 6207	Reo Pullman GEA61	B26F Bracebridge	12/29	12/29	6/46 to Brown

This very early photograph of three Hipwell vehicles shows in the foreground a 1929 Reo UT 6207 with stylish Bracebridge bodywork, one of two Reos which passed into the Brown fleet in June 1946.
Photo/ Omnibus Society – Roy Marshall

Reg No	Chassis & No	Body type	Date New	Date Acquired	Withdrawn
UT 8066	Maudslay ML3BC 4923	B38F Bracebridge	12/30	12/30	12/36 to Vernon Stoney Stanton
UT 9724	Bedford WLB 108137	B20F Willowbrook	12/31	12/31	8/34 to York Anwick
JU 698	Dennis Lancet 170102	B32F Willowbrook	6/32	6/32	6/46 to Brown
VJ 462	Dennis Lancet 170181	C32F Willowbrook	9/32	8/34	/38 to Brown, Donnington Wood
JU 3054	Dennis Lancet 170433	C32F Willowbrook	11/33	11/33	6/46 to Brown
JU 7225	Dennis Lancet 171005	DP38F Willowbrook	10/35	10/35	6/46 to Brown
UJ 2942	Commer Centaur 56028	B20F	3/34	7/36 ex PMT	7/38 to Keenan Carlingford, Eire
AAY 6	Dennis Lancet 2 175137	DP39F Willowbrook	12/36	12/36	6/46 to Brown
AAY 679	Bedford WTB 111077	C26F Duple	3/37	3/37	6/46 to Brown
AUT 194	Dennis Lancet 2 175353	DP39F Willowbrook	3/38	3/38	3/41 to W.D. & Gilbert, Tunbridge Wells
AUT 287	Bedford WTB 112073	C26F Duple	3/38	3/38	6/46 to Brown
RC 1525	Dennis Lancet 170419	C35F Willowbrook	8/33	5/34	6/46 to Brown
CUT 343	Bedford OWB 19582	B32F Duple	4/44	4/44	6/46 to Brown
DAY 146	Bedford OWB 30130	B32F Duple	9/45	9/45	6/46 to Brown

Photographed before entering service, Dennis Lancet JU 3054 with C32F Willowbrook bodywork dates from 1933. **Photo/ Omnibus Society – Roy Marshall**

Taken at the Willowbrook works in Loughborough in 1932, Dennis Lancet JU 698. **Photo/ Omnibus Society – Roy Marshall**

Wallace Dick Warner

Main Street, Markfield t/a W.D.Warner & Sons
Only vehicles and services acquired 1/48

Reg No	Chassis & No	Body type	Date New	Date Acquired	Withdrawn
AY 6358	Dennis	B20?	5/19	5/19	7/20 to goods
AY 6842	AEC Y	B26F	10/19	10/19	9/29 unknown
NR 1879	Maxwell Z1993	B Willowbrook	1/23	1/23	1/26 to lorry
NR 5919	Reo Speed Wagon 113159	B14	3/25	3/25	12/31 unknown
NR 2116	Crossley	B14	3/23	11/25 Ex Sibson & Mould, Enderby	8/26 to Greaves Leicester
NR 6391	Durant - Masco 3545	B20	5/25	-/28 ex Peach, Glenfield	c/28 unknown
VT 430	Leyland PLSC3 45901	B30	11/27	c/30 ex Cooke, Basford	by11/52 to Showman, Markfield

Seen before delivery during 1936, Warner's Dennis Lancet JU 7854 with bodywork by Willowbrook. It later passed to Brown's in January 1948. JU 7854 formed the basis of the first Dennis rebuild by Brown's during 1955.
Photo/ Omnibus Society – Roy Marshall

Reg No	Chassis & No	Body type	Date New	Date Acquired	Withdrawn
UT 3989	GMC T19 2650	B14	11/28	11/28	6/34 unknown
FP 2091	GMC T20 207729	B20 Willowbrook	11/28	by 11/33 ex Ainger, Oakham	9/33
UT 7012	Reo Pullman FB1333	B20 Wollowbrook	4/30	4/30	3/38 lorry to Warners
VX 1072	Reo Pullman FB1027	B20 Bush & Twiddy	6/29	5/34 ex Eastern National Omnibus Co (3507)	unknown
JU 7854	Dennis Lancet 2 175002	DP39F Willowbrook	1/36	1/36	1/48 to Brown
KF 4724	Leyland TS3 61819	C32F Burlingham	5/31	4/37 ex Ribble (1279)	c/40 to W.D.
AUT 694	Bedford WTB 112153	C26F Willowbrook	5/38	5/38	1/48 to Brown
DRF 530	Dennis Lancet 2 175066	DP39F Willowbrook	7/36	5/39 ex Berresford, Cheddleton	1/48 to Brown
WW 6814	Leyland TS1 60028	C30F Shearing c/36	8/28	6/44 ex Hughes, Bulkington	1/48 to Brown
TH 7165	Maudsley SF40 5319	DP36F Burlingham	4/36	c/40 ex Williams, Llandeilo	1/48 to Brown
FV 1550	Leyland TS2 61276	C32F Harrington c/39	c/31	5/41 ex Ferrington, Manchester	1/48 to Brown
CNR 362	Bedford OWB 11429	B32F Mulliner	12/42	12/42	1/48 to Brown
CNR 480	Bedford OWB 12531	B32F Roe	3/43	3/43	1/48 to Brown
DK 7378	Leyland TS1 61877	C32F Burlingham 3/39	c/31	10/44 ex Yelloway, Oldham	3/46 to Foster Glastonbury
DK 7379	Leyland TS1 61878	C32F Burlingham 3/39	c/31	c/44 ex Yelloway, Oldham	to Windredge, Son & Riley
GLL 939	Leyland LT8 302511	C35F Duple	3/39	5/46 ex MoS orig. BHS268 Smith, Barrhead	1/48 to Brown

John Henry Hill

45 Duncan Road, Leicester.

Acquired 1/52, but run separately as L.D.Brown, t/a J.H.Hill, Ashby Road, Markfield. The vehicles were transferred to the main Brown Fleet or sold during 1952 and 1953, the company forming one of the constituents of Browns Blue Coaches Limited on 1/7/54. In the interim coaches from the main Brown fleet ran "On Hire".

Reg No	Chassis & No	Body type	Date New	Date Acquired	Withdrawn
NR 7884	International			/25	/33
UT 9264	Bedford WLB	B20F	7/31	12/31 ex Whetton, Coalville	5/37 Kingham & Moore, Wombourne
ABC 495	Bedford WTB 110493	C26F	3/36	3/36	4/44 to Wright Southend
DRY 777	Bedford OWB 19576	B32F Duple Rebodied Duple Vista C29F 7/49	4/44	4/44	4/52 to Brown
FRY 684	Bedford OB 93365	C29F Duple	12/48	12/48	3/52 to Sharp, Boston
HBC 634	Bedford SB 1639	C31F Duple	6/51	6/51	6/53 to Brown
ERY 636	Bedford OB 47849	C29F Duple	4/47	4/47	c/52 to Williamson Leicester

William Parsons

Main Street,
Stanton-under-Bardon

Only vehicles and services aquired 8/53

Parsons took delivery of this Dennis Lancet in March 1950,it received a Yeates coach body, it was one of three vehicles which passed into the Brown fleet in August 1953. **Photo/ Omnibus Society Collection**

Reg No	Chassis & No	Body type	Date New	Date Acquired	Withdrawn
NR 8446	Ford T 12973849	B14	4/26	4/26	3/28 scrap
UT 2534	Chevrolet		3/28	3/28	unknown
UT 5907	Chevrolet LQ 58312	B14	9/29	9/29	7/32 to Sud weeks Devizes
UT 8607	Chevrolet 72983	B14	4/31	4/31	8/39 to Bishop Coalville (goods)
UT 9816	Bedford WLB 108262	B20F Willowbrook	12/31	12/31	8/39 scrap
JU 596	Bedford WLB 108344	B20F Willowbrook	5/32	5/32	8/46 to Machin, Ashby
JU 9211	Bedford WTB 110773	C25F Willowbrook	7/36	7/36	to mobile shop
AJU 877	Bedford WTB 111684	C25F Willowbrook	7/37	7/37	7/52 to Stephens, Rainham
UT 8888	Leyland Lion LT2 51444	B32F Duple	5/31	5/40 ex Vernon, Stoney Stanton	2/50 scrap
CNR 240	Bedford OWB	B32F Mulliner	10/42	10/42	2/52 unknown
DUT 149	Bedford OB 45396	C29F Plaxton	5/47	5/47	8/53 Hunt, Alford
FUT 77	Dennis Lancet III 759J3	C35F Yeates	3/50	3/50	8/53 to Brown
KNN 148	Bedford O 131446 rebuild	FC30F Plaxton	3/49	1/52 ex Wain, Mansfield	8/53 to Brown

Joseph Albert Rudin, Providence Cottage

Melbourne Road, Ibstock. T/A G. Rudin & Sons.

G. Rudin, passing to his son Joseph Albert Rudin 6/49. Vehicles and services taken over but premises not aquired.

Reg No	Chassis & No	Body type	Date New	Date Acquired	Withdrawn
NR 1072	Ford T 5819462	B14	5/22	5/22	1/27 to goods own lorry
NR 3826	GMC K16 21010	B20	4/24	4/24	12/29 to Gibson Barlestone
NR 7180	Ford 11278145	B14	8/25	8/25	2/28 to Blockley Heather
UT 2183	GMC		1/28	1/28	8/34 Unknown
UT 6210	GMC T60 60940	B26	11/29	11/29	by 9/36 to Farrow, Melton
UT 9764	Bedford WLB	B20P Willowbrook	11/31	11/31	9/37 to Huntley, Oakley
JU 4452	Dennis Lancet 170661	C32F Willowbrook	6/34	6/34	3/50 unknown
JU 7827	Dennis Lancet 171001	C32F Willowbrook	1/36	1/36	3/41 to W.D. & Batchelor, Barby
AJU 879	Bedford WTB 111619	C26F Duple	7/37	7/37	7/54 to Brown
BNR 631	Bedford WTB 19931	C26F Duple	7/39	7/39	7/54 to Brown
VJ 6068	Dennis Lancet 170459	C32F Willowbrook	c/34	11/40 ex Morgan Govilon rebody Yeates C32F 1/49	7/54 to Brown
ENR 294	Bedford OB 72926	C29F Duple	3/48	3/48	7/54 to Brown
AMS 257	Bedford OWB 23750	B30F SMT	1/45	3/50 ex Northern Roadways, Glasgow	7/54 to Brown
HJU 434	Bedford SB 7145	C33F Duple	1/52	1/52	7/34 to Brown

This Bedford WTB BNR 631 was delivered new to Rudins of Ibstock in June 1939, it was fitted with Duple bodywork, it passed into the Brown fleet in January 1954. **Photo/ Omnibus Society – J. F. Higham**

Supplied new to Rudin in March 1948, this Bedford OB ENR 294 with Duple Vista bodywork is seen outside Brown's Leicester Road, Ibstock premises. ENR 294 served in the Brown fleet until being withdrawn in October 1961.
Photo/ Roy Marshall

W. Windridge Sons to Windridge, Sons & Riley Ltd 6/33

Melbourne Road, Ibstock. t/a Comfy – owned by H. Bircher, Ibstock t/a Victory from 1948.
Acquired by L.D. Brown 1/8/56 and run separately using the Windridge name.
Absorbed by Browns Blue Coaches Ltd from 26/1/58.

Reg No	Chassis & No	Body type	Date New	Date Acquired	Withdrawn
NR 7661	Chevrolet R 6412	B14	11/25	11/25	8/28 to Taylor, Arksey
NR 7774	Chevrolet R 6829	B14	1/26	1/26	c11/27 to Davies Sutton-in-Ashfield
NR 9151	GMC K17 1257	B14	7/26	7/26	1/30 to Goods
FA 1820	Guy B	B20F Guy	5/24	3/27 ex Burton Corporation 1	3/29 to Goods
UT 1648	Reo		8/27	8/27	
UT 3466	Thornycroft A6 16389	B20	7/28	7/28	unknown
UT 4088	GMC T30 301928	B20	12/28	12/28	11/44 scrap
UT 6291	Maudsley ML3 4733	B32	1/30	/30	8/40 to W.D.
UT 7177	Reo Pullman GE195	B26	8/30	8/30	9/39 unknown
TF 6779	Leyland LT5 119	B32F Leyland	10/31	10/35 ex Leyland Motors	c/50 to Showman
UT 9811 No 4	Maudsley ML3A 4968	B32F Rainforth	12/31	12/31	9/47 to Ashmore Smethwick
JU 805 No 3	Maudsley ML3A 5069	B32F Rainforth	7/32	7/32	1/49 unknown
RB 6085 No 6	Leyland LT5 1296	B32 r/b Duple C32F	5/32 /37	c/34 Ex Stoppard Clay Cross	12/51 scrap
ANR 39 No 8	Bedford WTB 111690	C26F Duple	2/37	2/37	2/52 unknown
BNR 59	Leyland TS8 300302	C37F Plaxton	4/39	4/39	c/40 to W.D. & Brown 1946
CNR 364 No 1	Bedford OWB 11581	B32F Mulliner	1/43	1/43	/56 unknown
CUT 449 No 7	Bedford OWB 20951	B32F Duple	7/44	7/44	2/55 mobile shop
DK 7379 No 4	Leyland TS1 61878	C32F Burlingham (1939)	6/31	c/45 ex Warner, Markfield	c/51 unknown

During May 1947 Comfy Coaches placed this Leyland Tiger PS1/1 EAY 180 into service. Due to severe shortages in the immediate post war period a second hand rear entrance body built by Eastern Coachworks was fitted, seating 35. **Photo/ Omnibus Society Collection**

In December 1948 Comfy Coaches was sold to Hubert Bircher and renamed Victory Coaches, the body on EAY 180 was scrapped in 1950, and a new Yeates body was fitted. It is seen here in Eastern Boulevard, Leicester, on "Football Special" duty. **Photo/ Omnibus Society – Roy Marshall**

Reg No	Chassis & No	Body type	Date New	Date Acquired	Withdrawn
CK 4737 No 5	Leyland TS6 2643	C26R English Electric	4/33	10/40 ex Robin Hood, Nottingham	7/51 to Russell Coalville
HL 6376 No 9	Leyland LT5A 4366	B32F Roe	11/34	c/46 ex West Riding 385	-/54 to Mrs Roper Ibstock
EAY 180 No 2	Leyland PS1/1 462853	DP35R ex North Western Rebodied Yeates C35F 1950	5/47	5/47	1/58 to Brown
EUT 170 No 10	TSM K6LA7 9298	C32F Theale	7/48	7/48	7/57 to Forest Motors Mansfield
FAY 675 No 11	Bedford OB 97869	C29F Duple	2/49	2/49	1/58 Williamson, Leic
FUT 339 No 12	Bedford OB 125514	C29F Duple	12/49	12/49	1/58 to Brown
EUP 598 No 7	AEC Regent 06617285	H30/26R Northern Counties No	2/42	5/49 ex Stockton Corp 83	12/56 scrapped

Withdrawn after the initial purchase of Victory Coaches in August 1956, AEC Regent EUP 598 was originally an unfrozen chassis supplied to Stockton Corporation in 1942 Victory Coaches purchased the vehicle in 1949 for use on the busier sections of their route network. Although, the typical Northern Counties pre-war design with rounded domes was allowed to use up existing body stock. The interior was utility in design, although upholstered seats were fitted. **Photo/ Roy Marshall**

The last Bedford OB to be operated by Browns Blue was former Victory FUT 339, it passed into the fleet in January 1958, it carried a Duple Vista body. It is seen here in service with Victory in St. Margaret's Bus Station, Leicester.
Photo/ Roy Marshall

Reg No	Chassis & No	Body type	Date New	Date Acquired	Withdrawn
KAL 99 No 14	AEC Regal III 9621E 323	C33F Burlingham	10/48	3/51 ex Robin Hood Coaches Nottingham	1/58 to Brown
HAY 111 No 15	AEC Regal IV 9821 511	C41C Gurney Nutting	7/51	7/51	1/58 to Brown
ADO 619 No 16	AEC Regal 06624787	C35F Duple	6/46	c/51 ex Nightingale, Spalding	1/58 to Brown

Victory Coaches were taken over in August 1956 but operated as a separate company until January 1958, this 1951 AEC Regal IV No 15 HAY 111 with Gurney Nutting centre entrance bodywork was in many ways similar to the two AECs delivered to Browns Blue in the same year. It is seen here in Leicester Road, Ibstock.
Photo/Roy Marshall

Taken on Western Boulevard, Leicester, working a Football Special, AEC Regal ADO 619 with Duple bodywork dating from 1946 passed into the Browns Blue fleet in January 1958. **Photo/ John Shilcott Collection**

Most of the double deck fleet were parked at Copt Oak after the final day of service; this picture shows a line up of RT'S and Daimler CVD6 FNR 273 (far right) awaiting collection by their new owners. **Photo/ Ken Jubb**